WALKS FOR ALL AGES
WEST SUSSEX

WALKS FOR ALL AGES

WEST SUSSEX

KEITH McKENNA & SALLY DENCH

BRADWELL
BOOKS

Published by Bradwell Books
9 Orgreave Close Sheffield S13 9NP
Email: books@bradwellbooks.co.uk
© Keith McKenna & Sally Dench 2014

1st Edition

ISBN: 9781902674902

Print: Gomer Press, Llandysul, Ceredigion SA44 4JL

Design by: Erik Siewko Creative, Derbyshire.
eriksiewko@gmail.com

Photograph Credits: © Keith McKenna & Sally Dench

Maps: Contain Ordnance Survey data
© Crown copyright and database right 2014

Ordnance Survey licence number 100039353

The information in this book has been produced in good faith and is intended
as a general guide. Bradwell Books and its authors have made all reasonable
efforts to ensure that the details are correct at the time of publication
Bradwell Books and the author cannot accept any responsibility for any
changes that have taken place subsequent to the book being published
It is the responsibility of individuals undertaking any of the walks listed in
this publication to exercise due care and consideration for the health and
wellbeing of each other in the party. Particular care should be taken if you
are inexperienced. The walks in this book are not especially strenuous but
individuals taking part should ensure they are fit and able to complete the
walk before setting off.

Walk 1.	Chichester	2 miles	p.8
Walk 2.	Ferring	2¼ miles	p.14
Walk 3.	Hooksway	2¼ miles	p.18
Walk 4.	Steyning	2¼ miles	p.22
Walk 5.	Petworth	2½ miles	p.26
Walk 6.	Wisborough Green	2½ miles	p.30
Walk 7.	Loxwood	2¾ miles	p.34
Walk 8.	Lodsworth	2¾ miles	p.38
Walk 9.	Duncton	2¾ miles	p.42
Walk 10.	Ashurst	3 miles	p.46
Walk 11.	Ardingly	3¼ miles	p.50
Walk 12.	Singleton	3¼ miles	p.54
Walk 13.	Burpham	3½ miles	p.58
Walk 14.	Warninglid	3½ miles	p.62
Walk 15.	West Itchenor	4 miles	p.66
Walk 16.	Stoughton	4 miles	p.72
Walk 17.	Slindon	4½ miles	p.78
Walk 18.	Washington	4½ miles	p.82
Walk 19.	Hurstpierpoint	5¼ miles	p.88
Walk 20.	Arun Valley	5½ miles	p.92

INTRODUCTION

WEST SUSSEX, WITH ITS PREDOMINANT FEATURE OF THE
SOUTH DOWNS, IS LARGELY A QUIET AND BEAUTIFUL PLACE.
ITS COASTAL RESORTS, ALTHOUGH CONSIDERABLY DEVELOPED
DURING THE LAST CENTURY, REFLECT AN AIR OF REFINEMENT.

Its inland towns are desirable places to live and in 2006 Horsham was voted the second best place to live in the UK. Unfortunately the town is only 37 miles from London and such accolades only fuel the outward sprawl of urban development, which is increasingly felt in the north-east corner around Gatwick Airport.

Beyond this, however, lies the Sussex Weald and the lovely sight of the scarp edge of those dry, rolling hills so loved by poets and painters. Many famous authors have praised the beauty of the county and this in turn has brought more tourism; but apart from one or two downland 'honeypots' the tourists have not yet spoiled the very qualities they come to admire. It remains a benign landscape; neither dramatic nor threatening but always pleasing to the eye, in a very timeless and calming way.

Throughout the Weald and along the foot of the downs there are lots of pretty villages linked to each other by well-maintained footpaths and bridleways. Springs feed the streams that flow through these villages into the Sussex rivers of Adur, Arun, Rother and little Lavant. This makes for some lovely summer walks when the

"THEY ONLY KNOW A COUNTRY WHO ARE ACQUAINTED WITH ITS FOOTPATHS. BY THE ROADS INDEED, THE OUTSIDE MAY BE SEEN; BUT THE FOOTPATHS GO THROUGH THE HEART OF THE LAND."

wildflowers come out in profusion. But beware the winter when the same streams turn the clay of the Weald into ankle-deep mud! Our own general rule is to stay high on the downs in winter and leave the exploration of the Weald to the spring and summer months.

In choosing the 20 locations for this book we've tried to take all these things into account and to offer a variety of walks that show something of the coastline, the river valleys, the downland villages and, of course, the chalk hills of the South Downs. The Victorian nature writer Richard Jefferies famously wrote, 'They only know a country who are acquainted with its footpaths. By the roads, indeed, the outside may be seen; but the footpaths go through the heart of the land.' Nowhere is this more true than here in rural Sussex – where the roads do not flatter the countryside.

We hope that you enjoy every one of these walks as much as we did and that they may, perhaps, be the start of a lifetime of country walking.

Keith and Sally

CHICHESTER

Chichester is the county town of West Sussex, although its magnificent cathedral clearly makes it a city. But it is a small, user-friendly city whose centre is enclosed by the most intact Roman wall in southern England and this makes for a lovely walk.

Very little remains of the Roman town of Noviomagus apart from the two-metre thick walls and it seems that not long after their departure in 410 AD the town fell into decline leaving just North, South, East and West Streets radiating from the central market. Soon after the Roman departure it was occupied by Aelle, the first king of the South Saxons, and renamed after his son, Cissa. But it wasn't much of a town – just a few houses along the main streets – until Alfred the Great realised that the walls could be very useful in defending yourself against raiding Vikings. He rebuilt some of the walls and revived interest in the town.

Even so it wouldn't have seemed much of a prize to Roger de Montgomery who was handed the township in recognition of his courageous efforts in the Norman invasion of 1066. Soon afterwards he built a timber castle within the walls and with these new masters came new wealth. It was less than 40 years later when Bishop Ralph Luffa consecrated the magnificent cathedral. The cathedral is unusual in Britain in two respects; firstly in having a separate bell tower a few metres away from the main building, rather than integrated into it, and secondly for being the only medieval cathedral which is visible from the sea. In the south aisle a window in the floor affords a view of the remains of a Roman mosaic; a neat link over a thousand years of history.

Throughout the middle ages the city developed as a centre of trade and commerce – not all of it legitimate, since, with the proximity of the harbour, smuggling was big business hereabouts. It became important in the wool trade and bizarrely became famous for fish paste.

As you enter Priory Park (point 2) look to the right hand corner and you can clearly see the raised mound, which was the 'motte' of Montgomery's 11th century castle. The splendid Guildhall building you pass is all that remains of a much larger 13th century Franciscan friary. In 1749 the

trial of 7 smugglers was held here. After just two days they were all found guilty and executed the following afternoon. Several of the bodies were then hung in chains on the nearby downs 'to deter others'!

In the southwest quadrant thoughts turn to more peaceful matters in the Bishop's Palace Garden. There are water features, herbaceous borders and lots of mature specimen trees including the rare Gingko Biloba. A visit to the cathedral is, of course, a must and the café in the cloisters is one of the nicest places to stop for a break during the walk. If you are here in May or June look for the peregrine falcons on the cathedral turrets. They've been coming back here for over 12 years to nest and raise their chicks.

After the brief commercial bustle of South Street it's nice to wander back into the more sedate 'Pallant Quarter', which, like the city itself, is divided into four parts by streets called respectively North, South, East and West Pallant. There was formerly a wooden cross, at their junction. This is now the site of Pallant House, sometimes called Dodo House from the ostriches on the gateposts. The Gallery which it now houses is home to one of the best collections of 20th century British art in the country. It was winner of the 2007 Gulbenkian Prize - Britain's biggest single art prize.

THE BASICS

Distance: 2 miles: 3.2 km
Gradient: Level except for a few steps
Severity: Easy
Approx time to walk: 75 minutes
Stiles: None
Maps: OS Landranger 197 (Chichester & the South Downs); Explorer 120 (Chichester)
Path description: Urban paths and roads with some parkland
Start point: Cattle Market car park, Chichester, PO19 1JW (Grid Ref. SU 865046)
Parking: Pay & display public car park
Dog friendly: Not allowed in the Bishop's Palace Gardens
Public toilets: In the car park
Nearest food: Lots within a few minutes' walk

CHICHESTER WALK

This annual prize is awarded to the gallery with a 'track record of imagination, innovation and excellence'. The gallery's literature states, "It's not for boring old arts".

As you near the end of the walk, St John's Chapel is worth popping into. It's a rare example of the severe Georgian style of church, designed by James Elmes in 1813. At its peak it had a congregation of over 600 but, as with so many churches, numbers have declined and it passed into the Redundant Churches Fund around forty years ago.

THE WALK

1. From the car park entrance turn right to Eastgate Square then go left into East Street, heading towards the cathedral. In just 50m turn right into East Walls and, keeping to your right, follow the raised pavement up onto the city walls.

2. Follow the steps down into Priory Road, turn left and in just a few metres go right through a gate into Priory Park and aim across the grass towards the priory on the far side. Pass between the priory and the bowling green and climb the slope back onto the walls. Turn left to soon exit the park through a gate and turn right past the small shopping arcade to cross straight over North Street and climb back up onto the walls.

3. After passing County Hall leave the walls into Westgate and cross straight over into Avenue de Chartres. In just 75m turn left before a high wall following a sign to the Bishop's Palace Gardens. Enter through a gate in the wall and follow the path through the gardens to the far southeast corner to pass through a gap in the wall. Turn immediately left and leave the garden through a gate to reach the Bishop's Palace.

4. Turn right through The Gatehouse into Canon Lane and in 75m turn left down St. Richard's Walk towards the cathedral. On reaching the cloisters turn right past the cathedral shop and at the south-eastern corner turn right again

KEY

START POINT ●

through a gap in the wall and follow the passageway back to Canon Lane and go left through the gateway into South Street.

5. Turn left towards the Market Cross and take the first narrow road right into West Pallant. Follow this to the crossroads, with Pallant House ahead on the left, and cross straight over into East Pallant. Pass the Field & Fork Café and at the next crossroads go straight over into New Town to a T-junction.

6. Turn left past St. John's Chapel and continue up to East Street where a right turn will return you to Eastgate Square and the car park.

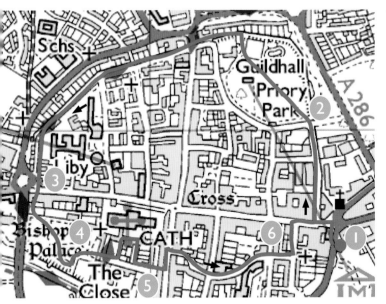

FERRING

The village of Ferring is the only coastal parish between Brighton and Littlehampton still bordered on both east and west by green fields.

The Bluebird café has been in existence for many years sometimes under a different name, including Martin's Retreat and The Lemon Tree. During the Second World War it was used by the army as a NAAFI canteen.

The shingle beach is home to many sea plants which have adapted in differing ways to deal with the harsh conditions. The large, impressive sea kale has a taproot, which grows as deep as two metres, giving access to fresh water and helping to anchor the plant in the unstable shingle. It is an edible member of the cabbage family, although perhaps best not picked along this route popular with dog walkers.

Different shells and other remains are evidence of the range of creatures living just off the coast. The distinctive black pods – mermaid's purse - are egg cases of thornback rays. Flat white cuttlebones are the skeletons of cuttlefish. These belong to the same family as squid and octopuses and recent studies have concluded that they are one of the most intelligent invertebrates. The Sussex coast is part of their breeding ground.

As the walk turns inland on the edge of the exclusive Kingston Gorse, it is said that a ghostly church bell can sometimes be heard. In the 17th century Kingston Chapel, which had long been threatened by the sea was finally lost.

To the north is the distinctive Highdown Hill. The earliest remains found here date from the Bronze Age and an Iron Age fort gives the hill its shape. An impressive tomb reflects a more bizarre aspect of its history. John Olliver ran the windmill that used

to be on top of Highdown. He was an eccentric figure, keeping his coffin on casters under his bed. On his death many flocked to see his coffin carried round the hill by people dressed in white and to hear the sermon, written by him, read by a young woman. Legend says that he is buried upside down.

The last part of the walk follows Ferring Rife, a very important local feature. 'Rife' is only used in this area of West Sussex and refers to a small stream running out to the sea. In 1994 it was designated a Site of Nature Conservation Importance (SNCI). An information board pictures many of the plants, butterflies, birds, etc that can be found on and around this rife. It is also plays a significant part in local flood management. In the mid-1980s, two storage lagoons were created to safeguard Ferring from flooding.

THE BASICS

Distance: 2¼ miles: 3.6 km

Gradient: Flat coastal walk

Severity: Easy

Approx time to walk: 60 minutes

Stiles: None

Maps: OS Landranger 197 (Chichester & the South Downs); Explorer 121 (Arundel & Pulborough)

Path description: Shoreline, quiet lanes and grassy footpaths

Start point: The Bluebird Café, Ferring, BN12 5QX (Grid Ref. TQ 091015)

Parking: Large free car park behind the Bluebird Café, Ferring

Dog friendly: Yes

Public toilets: In the car park and in the café

Nearest food: The Bluebird Café

FERRING WALK

1. From the car park walk behind the café to the western end of the car park and pass through a wooden kissing gate following the public footpath sign onto the shingle beach.

2. Cross the shingle to a grassy path and after 700m (10 minutes' walk) pass through a second kissing gate and turn right on a broad, hard surfaced drive, passing Lighthouse Cottage to your right. A third kissing gate leads onto a private road heading north and the views soon open out on either side as you cross Kingston Gorse. At the far side of the fields pass a First World War memorial and continue ahead on what is now a public road.

3. At the T-junction ahead, in front of a large flint wall, turn right following the public footpath sign into East Kingston Farm. Pass by Old Cottage with its pretty, low thatch and follow the path around as it begins to head east and then north around the field boundaries.

4. In the middle of the next large field, where there are fine views of Highdown Hill ahead of you, the footpath makes a sharp turn right to cross a substantial concrete bridge over Ferring Rife. On the other side of the rife meet a four-armed fingerpost and turn right, following the bank southwards.

5. Follow this pleasant path between the gardens of the houses and the watercourse all the way back to the car park and the welcoming sight of the Bluebird Café.

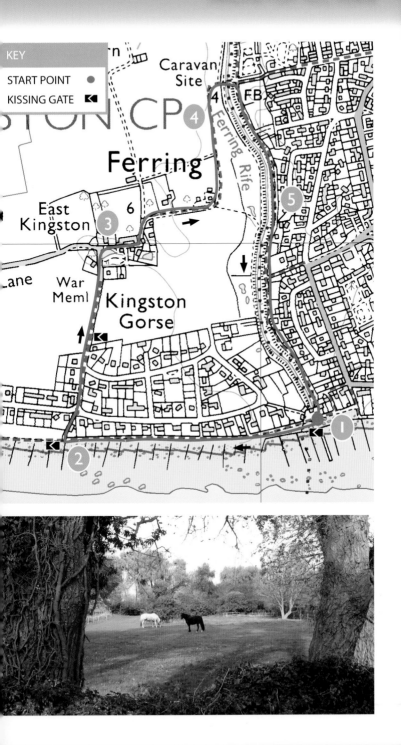

HOOKSWAY

THE MAJORITY OF THIS WALK IS WITHIN THE WEST DEAN ESTATE, WHICH IS OWNED AND MANAGED BY THE EDWARD JAMES FOUNDATION, A CHARITABLE EDUCATIONAL TRUST.

West Dean is recorded in the Domesday Book of 1086 as a hunting park. It was held for several centuries by the Earls of Arundel and Dukes of Norfolk, changing hands a number of times until William James bought the estate in 1891. At the turn of the 20th century the estate was well known for its large shooting parties, attended by King Edward VII and many other royal visitors. On William's death in 1912 the estate was inherited by his only son, Edward.

The estate is mainly farmed, providing a range of arable crops and grazed by cattle and sheep. However, one third is woodland and it is mostly through this that our walk takes place. Pheasant and partridge shoots are still an important part of the local economy and many young birds can be seen running around in the summer following their release. By the end of the shooting season on 1 February, only the wily few are left.

Part of the walk is through 'ancient woodland', meaning that the area has been continuously wooded since 1600 or before. It was from this date that fairly accurate estate maps began to be produced, showing areas of existing woodland, and widespread tree-planting began. Woods known to exist by that date were almost certainly natural in composition. This does not mean that such woodland has been undisturbed or unmanaged. The woods have been used for the production of hurdles for fencing and firewood and charcoal by coppicing.

Forestry remains an important commercial activity on the West Dean estate and piles of logs can be seen as the walk progresses. The severe storm of 1987 and another in 1990 devastated the woodland, blowing over historic 150-year-old beech trees as well as trees almost ready for commercial felling. Massive clearance and replanting were necessary and the estate is once again a successful woodland enterprise. As well as selling wood commercially, it fuels a biomass heating system that supplies all the heating and hot water needs of West Dean College (another part of the estate).

The South Downs Way is a 'national trail' running 100 miles from Winchester to Eastbourne. It follows the chalk ridge of the South Downs, one of the few routes passable by ancient Britons, above the densely forested valleys of The Weald and the dangers these presented. The trail is waymarked by distinctive acorn signs and is now a popular route for walkers, runners, cyclists and horse riders.

The Royal Oak at Hooksway is a delightful old building with a pretty garden. Dating from the 1400s it has long been a pub or alehouse. The grandson of one licensee described the life of his grandparents here at the end of the 19th century (a copy is available in the pub). William Woods was a gamekeeper but was attacked one day by poachers, which ended his career. Instead he became the licensee at the Royal Oak. He spent his time looking after the woodland and pastures, growing food and rearing animals to feed his family whilst his wife Martha ran the pub. She managed to stay 'open all hours', ignoring the licensing laws, by keeping the local police constable well supplied with free beer and produce from the farm.

Look out for the resident ghost of William 'Shagger' Shepherd who was a sheep rustler on the South Downs around 1680. A group of angry farmers chased him across the downs and he was eventually shot after taking refuge here in the pub.

THE BASICS

Distance: 2¼ miles: 3.6 km
Gradient: Short, steepish section of the South Downs Way
Severity: Short walk but with a moderate climb
Approx time to walk: 65 minutes
Stiles: None
Maps: OS Landranger 197 (Chichester & the South Downs); Explorer 120 (Chichester)
Path description: A broad 'bostal' (downland path) and good woodland paths
Start point: The Royal Oak, Hooksway, PO18 9JZ (Grid Ref. SU 815162)
Parking: Car park of the Royal Oak, by kind permission
Dog friendly: Yes
Public toilets: Only at the inn
Nearest food: The Royal Oak – please do pop in to say thanks for the parking!

HOOKSWAY WALK

1. Take the bridleway leading directly from the back of the car park following the blue arrow northwards along the valley floor. After 700m (10 minutes) pass through a gate into more open countryside. At a second gate the path begins to rise and becomes a 'restricted byway'.

2. Continue straight ahead along this classic chalk bostal past Buriton Farm and join the South Downs Way (SDW) coming in from your left. Just a few metres further on turn sharp right following the national trail. The bridleway climbs steadily into the trees and 250m after entering the trees you must look carefully to your right for a fingerpost indicating a bridleway glancing away to the right.

3. Turn right here off the SDW and continue to climb more gently before levelling off and starting a gentle descent through the trees. The path broadens and steepens then makes a half right as it passes several log piles in the woods.

4. Continue past Philliswood Barn and just after Philliswood Cottage return to the Royal Oak car park.

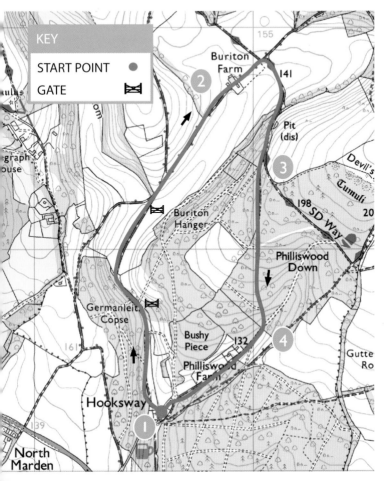

KEY

START POINT ●

GATE ⋈

155

Buriton Farm

141

2

Pit (dis)

Devil's

Tumuli

3

198 SD Way

20

ulus

graph ouse

Buriton Hanger

Philliswood Down

Germanleit Copse

161

Bushy Piece

132

Philliswood Farm

4

Gutte Ro

Hooksway

1

139

North Marden

STEYNING

STEYNING IS A MEDIEVAL MARKET TOWN WITH A RECORDED HISTORY GOING BACK OVER A THOUSAND YEARS.

The town's founding father was St. Cuthman who, after the death of his father in Wessex around 700 AD, brought his ageing mother here in what resembled a wheelbarrow. When he reached this piece of high ground between two streams the ropes holding the barrow broke and he took this as a sign from God that here he should settle and build a church.

You will see his statue as you leave the car park. It depicts him as a builder looking towards where his church stood. That original wooden building was replaced by the much larger St. Andrews Church we see today, constructed a mere 850 years ago. If the church is open do take a look.

As you walk up Church Street even a cursory glance at the buildings shows how much history there is here. On your right is 'The Forge' and it was here on 14th October 1651 that Charles II rested whilst his companion, Col. Gunter, had his horse re-shod. Little did they realise that Cromwell had troops based in Bramber less than a mile away.

At the end of Church Street on your right you will see a blue plaque on the wall of what was the Registrar's Office, commemorating Charles Parnell's marriage to Katherine O'Shea. On the opposite side of the High Street is the Stone House, the oldest residential building in town. The lower part was built in 1320 and the upper extension added some 200 years later.

You soon enter the Memorial Playing Fields with fine views of the downs and Chanctonbury Ring in the distance. Much of the rural part of this walk falls within the Steyning Downland Scheme where 160 acres of chalk downland have been designated for the benefit of wildlife and the local community. Known locally as the Horseshoe and the Rifle Range.

As you return to town you cross the millstream and get a glimpse of the old wheel. Court Mill produced animal feed - but closed in 1927. The stream feeding the wheel was diverted to the other side of the house about 20 years ago.

The road leading from here down to the High Street is Sir George's Place named after George Breach who founded a tannery (behind the Star Inn) in 1820. He was never knighted but was such a popular man that everyone called him 'Sir George'. During WW1 many of the sheepskin jerkins worn by our troops were made at his tannery.

On the High Street there are many buildings to admire but one of the most noticeable is the clock tower beneath which is Old Market House where George Fox, a founder of the Society of Friends (Quakers), held a meeting in 1655. In the past it was the Town Hall, Police Station and Fire Station. The clock itself was a gift from the Duke of Norfolk and was erected in 1860 although the building itself is much older.

THE BASICS

Distance: 2¼ miles: 3.6 km

Gradient: One very gentle climb and descent

Severity: Easy

Approx time to walk: 55 minutes

Stiles: None

Maps: OS Landranger 198 (Brighton & Lewes); Explorers 121 (Arundel & Pulborough) and 122 (Brighton & Hove)

Path description: Parkland, good footpaths and road surfaces

Start point: Opposite St Andrews Church, Steyning, BN44 3XZ (Grid Ref. TQ 179113)

Parking: 'Fletchers Croft' car park opposite St Andrews Church

Dog friendly: On leads in the town

Public toilets: By the Steyning Centre in the car park and in the High Street

Nearest food: Loads to choose from in the High Street

STEYNING WALK

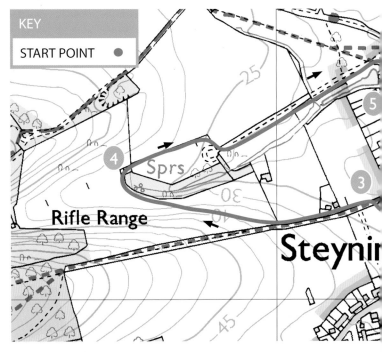

Finally take a look to your right at the Chequer Inn. The height of the archway clearly shows this was built to allow a coach & driver to enter and this was indeed an important 'posting' stop on the London to Worthing coach route.

Time now for refreshment; a provision at which the town excels.

The Walk

1. From Fletchers Croft car park walk back towards the church and turn left alon Church Street. On reaching the High Street cross straight over and walk past th White Horse Inn to reach White Horse Square and turn right into Charlton Stree

2. In just 30m turn left by the police station onto the Memorial Playing Field. Cros the field, past the children's play area, to the far right hand corner and ex through a kissing gate onto a rough track.

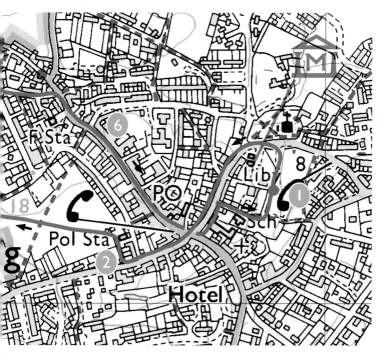

. Turn left heading uphill and in 200m reach a second kissing gate and turn right through a third gate into an open area called 'Butterfly Land'. Follow the clear grassy path ahead, which starts off level and then descends into the valley.

. At the bottom follow the path right around the trees to almost reverse direction and head back towards town. The grassy path gives way to a hard surface between elder and blackberry bushes and nearing the town passes through a wooden gate. Immediately after this, and before reaching the thatched cottage, turn right on a narrower path through the bushes. As you cross the course of the old millstream there are views of Court Mill, with its old waterwheel, to the right.

. On reaching the public road ahead turn left downhill passing Sir George's Place to reach the Star Inn.

. Turn right and walk up the High Street, admiring the many different timber-framed buildings in this medieval town, and return to the crossroads by the White Horse Inn. Turn left along Church Street and this time, opposite the Norfolk Arms, turn right down a passageway to return to the car park.

PETWORTH

Although best known for its splendid house and deer park, Petworth has a tradition that goes back much further. Every 20th November on St Edmunds Day, they hold a fair in Market Square and they've been doing so for 825 years.

It started during the reign of Richard the Lionheart and was then an eight or nine-day affair. One can only imagine the goings-on; today it's rather more of a children's fun fair.

The cobbled Lombard Street is delightful and gets its name from a part of northern Italy called Lombardy. It was from there that the goldsmiths and merchant bankers of London originated and it may well have been Henry de Percy (see below) who gave the street its name since he was known to have borrowed heavily from the Lombard Society.

At the top of the street is St Mary's Church and you might expect such a prominent church

to have an impressive spire – and indeed it once did so. An early wooden spire was replaced in 1827 by a beautiful brick structure designed by Charles Barry, architect of the Houses of Parliament. Bizarrely, in 1947 it was declared unsafe by the building inspectors and was demolished. The not so pretty present tower was completed in 1953. The 1851 gas lamp standard in the road to your right was also designed by Sir Charles and fortunately, has fared rather better than his spire.

The site of the present Petworth House was originally occupied by a fortified manor

founded by Henry de Percy, who was born in Petworth in 1273. Charles Seymour, 6th Duke of Somerset – the so-called 'proud duke' – rebuilt the house we see now in 1688. For the past 250 years the house and the estate have been in the hands of the Wyndham family – currently Lord Egremont. He and his family live in the south wing, allowing much of the remainder to be open to the public.

t was the 3rd Earl of Egremont who, at the end of the 18th century, added greatly to he art collection, which now contains paintings by Holbein, Reynolds, Gainsborough, Rembrandt and 19 oils by J.M.W. Turner, who spent a lot of time here.

The 700-acre park itself was designed by garden design guru Capability Brown, who shifted 70,000 tons of soil and clay to make the 'natural' vistas so beautifully painted by Turner. It is now home to the largest herd of fallow deer in England, numbering over 1,000 bucks and does. The bucks 'rut', with a fearful roar, at the end of October and the awns are born eight months later. Fallows are easily distinguished from other deer by the palmate (flattened) antlers and the black and white patch on their rump.

THE BASICS

Distance: 2½ miles: 4 km

Gradient: Very gentle slopes

Severity: Easy

Approx time to walk: 80 minutes

Stiles: None

Maps: OS Landranger 197 (Chichester & the South Downs); Explorer 133 (Haslemere & Petersfield)

Path description: Parkland with some town roads

Start point: Town centre car park, GU28 0AN (Grid Ref. SU 976215)

Parking: Pay & display public car park

Dog friendly: Permitted in the park – but on a lead through the town

Public toilets: In the car park

Nearest food: Cafés in the shopping arcade next to the car park

PETWORTH WALK

1. Walk to the north-eastern end of the car park, pass the toilet block and enter the shopping arcade. After passing the Bay Tree Bakery exit into the High Street and walk up into Market Square with the Star Inn and Leconfield Hall to your left.

2. Keeping to the right-hand side of the square, walk up into the cobbled Lombard Street. At the top of the street cross the road carefully to St Mary's Church and turn right to follow the pavement as it swings left around the church into North Street. You must cross the road again here and walk downhill for just 50m before crossing back over to enter the courtyard.

3. Follow the National Trust signs into Petworth Park through the courtyard and at the bottom of the yard turn left to pass through the Cowyard Tunnel to the ornate iron gate leading into open parkland. Turn half left on an obvious track going slightly away from the house, and in a few minutes, when the lake comes into view, head for the left-hand corner of it.

4. Follow the path around the lakeside and at the south-west corner, where the path divides, take the right fork. The gravelly path climbs gently now for 350m and then starts to level off as you approach a line of trees and a high deer fence to your left. Look carefully here for a well-trodden grassy path going to the right over a rise and down into the valley. Follow this back down towards the lake.

5. At the bottom of the valley, on reaching a metal fence, turn left to follow the path around the northern end of the lake. Just after rounding the top of the lake turn left on a cleared grass path going uphill to a splendid viewpoint. At the top of the rise reach a junction of five paths and pause to admire a magnificent view of the whole park. If you have not yet seen the famous deer you will almost certainly do so from here!

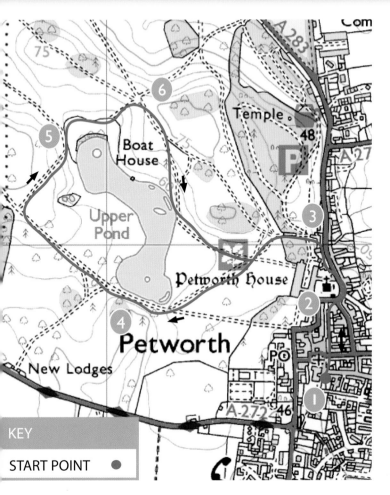

KEY

START POINT ●

Turn right now, heading just slightly uphill, and as the path levels off take the right-hand fork to drop back down to the lakeside. As the house comes back into view turn left towards it, aiming to the left side where the tunnel will return you into the town. Retrace your steps back to the arcade and car park.

WISBOROUGH GREEN

THIS WALK TAKES US INTO THE LOW WEALD OF SUSSEX, A BROAD LOW-LYING CLAY VALE.

Inland transport was a major problem in Britain during the Industrial Revolution with the growing need to move greater volumes of goods and raw materials over longer distances. The roads of the time were inadequate and no more so than in Sussex, where many were described as 'bottomless' during winter months. A Dictionary of Sussex Dialect published in 187 included 30 different words for mud – including ike, clodgy, gubber, slub, smeery, stu and swank.

The 23-mile Wey and Arun Canal was built between 1813 and 1816 to link the Rivers We (to the north) and Arun (which this walk follows), creating a route between London an the south coast. During the Napoleonic Wars it was an important means of transportin military supplies to the fleet at Portsmouth, later carrying coal, chalk, lime and farr produce. One important shipment was bullion from Portsmouth to the Bank of England transported with a guard of four Redcoats. Faster rail travel soon ended the use of canal and this one was sadly abandoned in the 1870s.

The part of the canal this walk follows was called the Arun Navigation, linking Pallinghar in the south to New Bridge just north of here. Like many major building projects of today the project ran over budget. It cost £16,000 rather than the £10,000 allowed – in today' money, almost £1.5 million compared to an expected £934,000.

In 1868, a Mr and Mrs Dashwood journeyed along the canal in their boat Caprice, writin a charming narrative of their experiences, including comments on the section covere by this walk. 'We reached the first lock, which was opened for us whilst we watched th lock-keeper's wife and two pretty daughters making butter in the early morn. Thoug flat, the meadows on each side presented a truly English picture – with cattle dotte about here and there and the banks of the canal clothed with wildflowers of every hu and colour.'

The canal they followed is now virtually non-existent here and can only just be seen a a scar across the fields. The walk takes us to Lording's (also known as Orfold) Lock an aqueduct. Here there was a waterwheel, the original long gone, that lifted water from the river into the canal. This wheel was unusual in its construction and much research was needed to discover how it looked and operated. A replica wheel is now in place and can be seen working some weekends: check www.weyandarun.co.uk.

On leaving the canal, the walk crosses remote farmland. Many of the old hedges are remnants of the woodland that once covered much of the Low Weald. Early farmers cleared small fields from the forest, leaving strips of woodland known locally as 'shaws' or 'rews'. An ancient hedgerow is rich in different native species such as hawthorn, blackthorn, dogwood and buckthorn and provides an important habitat for wildlife.

The Limeburners Inn was apparently once a row of cottages occupied by men who worked the kilns to produce lime. This was an important raw material in agriculture, improving the structure and quality of the soil. Here limekilns would have used chalk transported

on the canal to produce lime for the local farmers. William Cobbett observed the area during his Rural Rides in the 1820s: 'Soon after quitting Billingshurst I crossed the River Arun, which has a canal running alongside it. At this point there are large timber and coal yards, and kilns for lime. This appears to be a great receiving and distributing place.' Very different to the quiet rural location we enjoy today.

THE BASICS

Distance: 2½ miles: 4 km

Gradient: Mostly level walk with just two gentle hills

Severity: Easy – but liable to flooding in wet weather

Approx time to walk: 75 minutes

Stiles: Seven

Maps: OS Landranger 197 (Chichester & the South Downs); Explorer 134 (Crawley & Horsham)

Path description: Some narrow, rough sections which will be muddy after rain; best enjoyed in a spell of dry weather

Start point: Limeburners Inn, RH14 9JA (Grid Ref. TQ 072254)

Parking: Free roadside lay-by parking adjacent to the inn car park

Dog friendly: On a lead through the paddocks

Public toilets: Wisborough Green village or at the inn

Nearest food: The Limeburners Inn or teashop in Wisborough Green

1. Walk down the road past the inn and cross carefully as soon as you can. Take the first footpath right down a tarmac drive and just before the entrance to Guildenhurst Place look for a footpath through the hedge to the right and cross the stile into an open field.

2. Two more stiles lead over the rise and downhill into the river valley. Cross a wide farm bridge over the river and in a

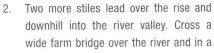

further 50m turn left at the four-armed fingerpost, following the Wey South Path. Cross a stream and follow the tree line on your right for 700m (about 10 minutes) to reach a stile leading into a wood.

3. The path now follows a narrow raised embankment between the river to your left and the course of the old canal to your right. It exits the wood over a stile and turns sharply right, away from the river. Follow the hedge line to your right for a further 500m and cross a stile to the fascinating arrangement of Lording's Lock and its waterwheel.

4. Leave the lock on a bridge over the river and at the kissing gate take the left fork in the path. It curves gently left and, on passing through a metal gate, begins to climb gently up the left side of a field. At the brow of the hill, near the corner of the field, look for a fingerpost on your left beneath a large

oak and follow the path quite steeply downhill. This can be muddy and slippy.

5. Follow the path over a stile along the valley floor and, after briefly rejoining the riverbank, turn left on a concrete bridge over a stream and then almost immediately right following a yellow footpath arrow. Follow the lakeside path to the boathouse and here turn left following the footpath up a grassy track between two hedgerows.

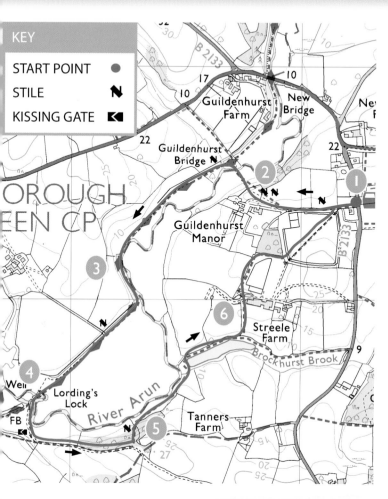

KEY

START POINT ●
STILE N
KISSING GATE ◧

6. After passing a splendid 'tree house' go to the left of two barns and turn right over a plank bridge. Follow this clearly marked path through two gates and then across an open field besides paddocks. A gate leads out of the field and onto the drive where we began the walk. Turn right and then left to the Limeburners Inn.

LOXWOOD

In 1868, Loxwood was described as a 'small place, but boasts of a neat clean inn close by the canalside'. The Onslow Arms is a typical canalside pub, which would have been used by those building the canal as well as by bargees and other travellers.

The walk starts from the Wey and Arun Canal Trust visitor centre, which is well worth a visit (their website www. weyandarun.co.uk. also provides a wealth of information on the canal and its restoration).

In 1970 a canal society was formed, becoming a charitable trust in 1973. It aims to restore the 23 miles of the Wey and Arun Canal, re-creating the water link between London and the South Coast – 'London's lost route to the sea.' The Trust has reached agreement with landowners that restoration can take place over half the canal's length. Restoration is both complicated and expensive. So far 21 bridges have been rebuilt, 2 aqueducts reconstructed, 11 locks restored and several miles of canal bed cleared and dredged. Further challenges remain; some parts of the old canal have now almost totally reverted to farmland and will need to be rebuilt completely.

The Trust runs boat trips along the restored part of the canal at Loxwood. They have three boats – 'Zachariah Keppel' is named after the contractor originally engaged to build the canal and 'Josias Jessop' after the engineer who surveyed the route. The Wiggonholt Association sponsored their newest boat, 'Wiggonholt'.

One amazing project was the re-building of the bridge under the road besides the Onslow Arms. This involved building a new lock, lowering part of the canal and building a new bridge, during which the main road through the village was closed. The project cost nearly £2m, which was entirely raised by the Canal Trust.

Walking along the canal it can be seen that the surrounding area is also being restored, wildflowers have been planted and hedges layered in the traditional way. Brewhurst Lock is one of those that have been restored and Brewhurst Bridge was re-built in 1994 in its original style. Baldwin's Knob is named after the area behind here. 'Knob' is an old Sussex word for a small hill and Baldwin was probably the name of the local farmer or landowner.

Drungewick aqueduct and the neighbouring bridge were rebuilt between 2000 and 2003. In 1905 Drungewick Bridge was in such a poor state that it was closed and the canal ran through a culvert under the road, to allow drainage and prevent any build up of water. Only a small gap in the hedge showed where the bridge had been until the reconstruction began.

The Farleycopse herd of charolais cattle was established in 1976 with the purchase of two in-calf heifers. Since moving to Drungewick Hill Farm in 1984 the herd has expanded to 45 pedigree cows. The distinctive creamy white charolais were the first continental breed of cattle introduced to Britain. They are large muscled with the bulls weighing over one ton. They grow fast and provide excellent meat.

The attractive hamlet of Brewhurst contains a number of listed buildings. The mill has been in existence since at least 1500 although a major fire in 1890 destroyed the upper floors. It has two waterwheels. A second one had to be added, as the original was too low to operate effectively when the river was in flood. The mill stopped operating commercially in 1968. It is now a listed building and privately owned, although open to the public on occasions.

THE BASICS

Distance: 2¾ miles: 4.4 km

Gradient: One very short climb on a country lane

Severity: Easy

Approx time to walk: 75 minutes

Stiles: None

Maps: OS Landranger 197 (Chichester & the South Downs) and 187 (Dorking & Reigate); Explorer 134 (Crawley & Horsham)

Path description: Good canal towpaths with some pine forest paths

Start point: The Wey and Arun Canal Trust visitor centre, Loxwood RH14 0RD (Grid Ref. TQ 041311)

Parking: Free car park by visitor centre

Dog friendly: Yes

Public toilets: Only at the inn

Nearest food: The Onslow Arms, Loxwood

LOXWOOD WALK

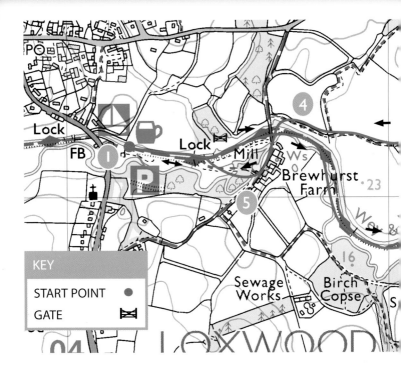

KEY

START POINT ●

GATE ⋈

1. From the car park walk onto the canal side and head eastwards along the towpath. Pass Brewhurst Lock, whose gates appear to be the wrong way round, and at a crossroads by the bridge continue straight ahead through a gate. Follow this pleasant route past the lock at Baldwin's Knob (partially funded by Footprints of Sussex) and in a further 1 km reach the Drungewick Aqueduct.

2. Cross the aqueduct and turn left along the public road to cross a stream in the dip and climb the other side. At the top of the hill take the first footpath left through Farleycopse Farm – home of the splendid Charolais beef herd. The concrete track gives way to a gravel drive heading into the trees. Some 200m into the trees, on reaching a small pond, turn right off the main track.

3. Just after the pond, at the next path junction, continue straight ahead through tall pine trees crossing a small stream on a plank bridge and eventually emerge into an open field. Follow the fingerpost ahead to the tree line opposite

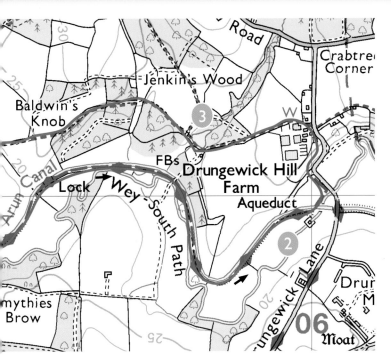

and follow the edge of the field to meet the northern bank of the canal.

4. On reaching a tarmac road turn left over Brewhurst Bridge to cross the canal and continue straight ahead away from the canal over two smaller bridges to reach the splendid house called 'Brewhurst'. Walk past

the open barn and on reaching 'The Mill' on your right turn right following the footpath fingerpost.

5. Walk past the mill with its old iron wheel and cross a bridge over the weir to enter an open field besides the millstream. Follow the meander around to climb a small bank back onto the canal towpath and turn left to return to the car park and the welcoming sight of the lovely gardens at the Onslow Arms.

LODSWORTH

LODSWORTH IS A DELIGHTFUL VILLAGE WITH MANY ATTRACTIVE BUILDINGS. MOST OF THE COTTAGES ALONG THE STREET ARE 16TH AND 17TH CENTURY, ALTHOUGH REPAIRS AND ALTERATIONS HAVE CHANGED THEIR APPEARANCE.

At the beginning of the 20th century, Lodsworth was a self-supporting community with a range of shops and businesses, including a blacksmith and other crafts, a post office and general store and, later, a garage. The last shop and post office closed in 1988.

In 2005 there was overwhelming support for bringing back a village shop. Funding was partly raised by local people buying shares in the store and some grants were obtained. An eco-friendly, not-for-profit shop – the Lodsworth Larder – finally opened in 2009. This sells a wide range of fresh produce and groceries and also runs a postal service. The Larder has won a number of awards, both for the building itself and for the business. In 2012 it was named the Daily Telegraph Magazine 'Best Corner Shop'.

The Hollist Arms was originally called the Poyntz Arms after the family that owned the surrounding land. Hasler Hollist inherited a large estate in Lodsworth from his aunt in the 1830s and, on acquiring the pub, changed its name to his. The magnificent chestnut tree in front of the pub was planted to celebrate Queen Victoria's diamond jubilee in 1897.

The Hollists and Dennetts were the main landowners in Lodsworth during the 19th and early 20th centuries. Both families had a sense of community responsibility and encouraged many local activities. Each showed their standing in society by having special pews in the church for themselves and their servants. The last member of the Dennett family died in 1962, ending 180 years living in the village.

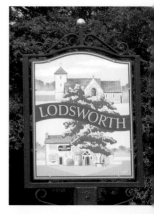

To mark their Silver Wedding in June 1890 Colonel and Mrs Hollist invited everyone in Lodsworth, Easebourne and Tillington, who had been married twenty-five years or more, to come to tea. Nearly 100 couples accepted the invitation. One of the features of the afternoon was a cricket match –

Lodsworth versus Easebourne. Lodsworth won and each member of the team was presented with a cap in dark and light blue stripes. Just north of the church, slightly off our route, is St Peter's Well. This was a place visited by medieval pilgrims – the water was said to have healing qualities, being especially good for bad eyes. It has been suggested that St Peter's Church was originally built as a chapel for these pilgrims.

Towards the end of the walk the path passes between blackberry bushes. It was believed that these should not be picked after Michaelmas Day at the end of September. Legend tells us that it was on this day that the devil was kicked out of heaven. He landed in a prickly bramble bush and cursed the fruit, spitting on them (or worse) and making them unsuitable to eat. Every year he renews his curse by spitting on each bush.

The artist and illustrator Ernest H. Shepard spent the last 20 years of his life living in the house called 'Woodmancote' and a blue plaque reminds us of this. He was awarded the Military Cross for bravery during World War II. Although contributing to many publications he is now mainly remembered for his illustrations bringing to life characters such as

THE BASICS

Distance: 2¾ miles: 4.4 km

Gradient: One short steep section, and gentle climb back to the village

Severity: Easy

Approx time to walk: 70 minutes

Stiles: Two

Maps: OS Landranger 197 (Chichester & the South Downs); Explorer 133 (Haslemere & Petersfield)

Path description: A forest trail, then beside hedgerows and open fields

Start point: The Lodsworth Larder village store, Lodsworth, GU28 9BZ (Grid Ref. SU 927231)

Parking: Village store car park next to the Hollist Arms, by kind permission

Dog friendly: Yes

Public toilets: Only at the inn

Nearest food: The Hollist Arms or take-away snack from the award-winning store

LODSWORTH WALK

Winnie-the-Pooh, Eeyore, Piglet, Ratty and Toad in the Pooh books of A.A. Milne and Kenneth Grahame's The Wind in the Willows. In 1962 he designed the original cover for the Lodsworth parish magazine and this continued to be used for many years after his death.

THE WALK

1. From the car park turn left along The Street, through the village. After the last cottage on the right, turn right following the footpath fingerpost downhill through a gate towards the tall trees. Cross the stream on a plank bridge and continue ahead as a footpath joins from the left.

2. At a fork in the path keep right to reach a three-armed fingerpost on the edge of the wood and turn left. Follow the fence line on your left, keeping about 15m into the field, to reach a second fingerpost and turn right. In just 20m turn left through a metal gate and cross the stone bridge over the River Lod.

3. About 25m into the wood, at a third three-armed fingerpost, turn right to follow the bridleway uphill. At the top of a steep little climb reach a T-junction and turn right on the footpath going downhill. The path stays high above the steep valley of the river, passing several beautiful beech trees, before crossing two stiles to join the drive leading away from Woodbarn Cottage.

4. At the end of the drive turn right along the quiet lane to cross the river and, just beside the Halfway Bridge Inn, turn right up the tarmac bridleway past Custard Cottage. Passing Cowdray Barns the trail becomes a narrower grassy path between blackberry bushes (come here in September for a feast) before

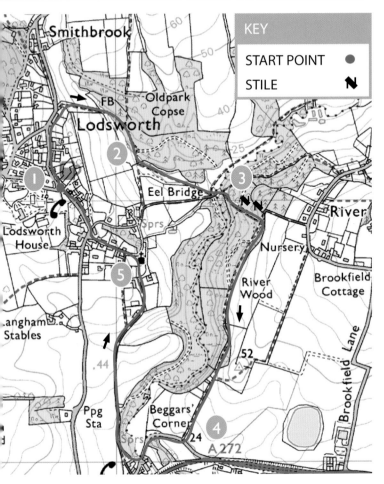

KEY

START POINT ●

STILE 🏃

opening out into a large field. Follow the fence line on the right now, to pass to the right of the cottages ahead, and reach a gravel drive leading past Manor Farm to the churchyard.

5. Walk through the churchyard under the monkey-puzzle tree and exit through the lychgate to continue straight up Church Lane into the village. At the main road turn right and follow this back to the Village Store car park.

DUNCTON

DUNCTON MILL TAKES ADVANTAGE OF ONE OF THE MANY
CHALK STREAMS RUNNING FROM THE FOOT OF THE DOWNS
THE MILL WAS ONCE USED FOR MILLING CORN AND CLOTH.

It is now a commercial trout farm and fishery raising both brown and rainbow trout. These are sold to restock large reservoirs and small syndicate waters, as well as stocking the large lakes for fishing on site. The fishery also has facilities for hosting weddings, conferences and other special events.

Duncton was famous for the old custom of 'wassailing', which continued here until the 1920s. Early in January the wassailers would visit each house in the village with an orchard and, surrounding the trees, they would chant a rhyme and blow their horns. Much cider was drunk on these occasions. The ceremony drove away any evil spirits lurking in the trees and ensured a good apple crop for the coming season.

The current house at Burton Park dates from 1828, following the partial destruction of an older house by fire. During the Second World War it was occupied by the army. The house and some of the grounds were then sold to St Michael's School and it remained a boarding school for girls until being bought in the early 1990s by three developer companies. The house was converted into private apartments and new dwellings were built in the immediate gardens. The park is privately owned and the house is a Grade I listed building.

Beside the house is the tiny church of St Richard, one of the smallest in Sussex, and still in regular use. Originally built around 1075, it has been altered and restored over the centuries. It is well worth pausing to visit, not least to admire the unusual wall painting reputed to be of St Wilgefortis, also known as St Uncumber. This unfortunate young woman was the daughter of a Portuguese nobleman who had been promised in marriage by her

father to a pagan king. To prevent the wedding Uncumber took a vow of virginity and prayed that she would be made repulsive. Her prayers were answered – she sprouted a luxurious beard, which quickly ended the engagement. Her father was so angry he had her crucified! During the 14th century she was venerated by those seeking relief from tribulations, especially by women who wished to be 'disencumbered' of abusive husbands.

This walk takes in small parts of two waymarked trails. The Serpent Trail runs from Haslemere to Petersfield. These towns are only 15 miles (25 km) apart by road, but the trail takes a 64-mile serpentine route across many areas of heathland. A guide can be downloaded from www.southdowns.gov.uk providing information about the plants and creatures to be found in these important habitats.

West Sussex has been the home to many authors and featured in many novels. The West Sussex Literary Trail traces a pretty 55-mile (88 km) route from Horsham to Chichester and the trail guide brings to life the many literary connections along the way. (See www.westsussexliterarytrail.co.uk).

THE BASICS

Distance: 2¾ miles: 4.4 km

Gradient: One short, easy climb from the fishery; otherwise flat

Severity: Easy

Approx time to walk: 80 minutes

Stiles: None

Maps: OS Landranger 197 (Chichester & the South Downs); Explorer 121 (Arundel & Pulborough)

Path description: Hard surface drives and good footpaths

Start point: Cricketers Inn, Duncton, GU28 0LB (Grid Ref. SU 960170)

Parking: Lay-by in front of the Cricketers Inn, Duncton

Dog friendly: Yes

Public toilets: Only at the inn

Nearest food: Cricketers Inn

DUNCTON WALK

The pub at Duncton was originally called the Swan but was renamed the Cricketers by John Wisden, who bought it in 1867. He played cricket for Kent, Middlesex, Sussex and England and launched the famous Wisden Cricketers' Almanac. Duncton was the birthplace of two other famous cricketers, both of whom played for Sussex and England. James 'Jemmy' Dean – known as the Sussex Ploughboy – leased the pub for some time and died there on Christmas Day 1881, while sitting in the inglenook with a pint of beer. Jem Broadbridge also contributed to Sussex cricket becoming County Champions in the 1820s. He would walk from Duncton to Brighton, a distance of over 25 miles, just to play in matches.

THE WALK

1. From the lay-by walk northwards along the grass verge beside the road and take the first bridleway right. Follow this tarmac driveway over a stream and up to Duncton Fisheries. After admiring the rainbow trout in this beautiful spot, continue up the drive and in 75m turn left following a bridleway uphill through the trees.

2. Pass by an old orchard before the track opens out with fine views to the north and take the next bridleway left down the side of a large open field. This path crosses the headwaters of the first of the Burton Mill Ponds before an iron gate leads into another open field and onto the drive past Burton Park Mansion.

3. On reaching the small church of St Richard take the bridleway left and follow this stony track northwards towards an isolated farmhouse. In 300m turn right following the 'Serpents Trail' towards a large clump of trees. Pass besides Black Pond to emerge through a kissing gate onto the tarmac drive beneath a splendid sweet chestnut tree. Here turn right back towards the mansion.

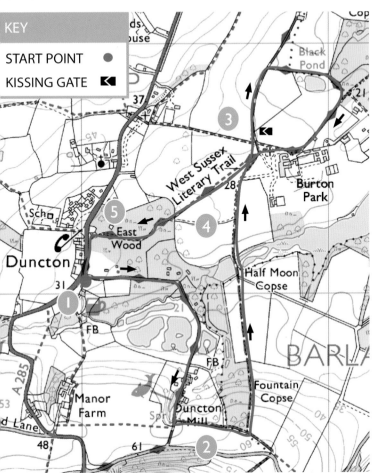

KEY

START POINT ●

KISSING GATE ◤◣

4. On passing St Richard's Church, continue along the drive for a further 50m and fork right following the yellow footpath arrow on a narrow path between two fences (this is also the West Sussex Literary Trail). On reaching the driveway once more turn right and follow this through the trees to the main road.

5. Turn left and walk down the grass verge on the left side of the road to the welcoming sight of the Cricketers Inn.

ASHURST

ALTHOUGH THE NAME SIMPLY MEANS A 'HILL OF ASH TREES' YOU ARE MORE LIKELY TO BE IMPRESSED BY THE MAGNIFICENT OAK TREES TOWARDS THE END OF THIS WALK.

The first point of interest is, of course, the church of St James with some notable features. It houses an extraordinary vamping horn hanging on the wall of the nave. Such things were probably used by someone in the choir to liven up the hymns although one theory about their use refers to deaf vicars! Although dated 1770 this is actually a replica.

In the graveyard you will find a tall wooden cross marking the grave of Margaret Fairless Barber, whose pen name was Michael Fairless. She died in 1901 and it was only later that her book The Roadmender was published. It is a series of meditations on the road to heaven and became a wild success, being reprinted an amazing 31 times in ten years. This whole area became known as 'Roadmender Country'.

Another, perhaps better known parishioner was Sir Laurence Olivier whose funeral service was held here in 1989. He is, of course, buried in Westminster Abbey.

The striking Withyfield Cottage was completed in the spring of 2011 by Ben Law using local timber, clay, straw and cedar shingles and is a superb testament to contemporary green building practice. The roof is insulated with eight inches of sheep's wool and the solar panels provide both heating and hot water. It's available for holiday lets throughout the year.

Soon after the cottage you'll walk under the oaks we mentioned earlier. They are predominantly pedunculate oak – a species that clearly grows well in Ashurst since sales of oak were recorded here as far back as 1357, with buyers coming from all over the country for the precious timber. In his poem 'Sussex'

Rudyard Kipling wrote: 'Huge oaks and old, the which we hold no more than Sussex weed.'

The walk finishes at The Fountain, which first became an inn under the sign of the Red Lion in 1788, and adopted the name Fountain about 50 years later. An extra wing was added on the north side in the early 1800s and, at the same time, the facade was altered from its original timber-framed appearance to the Georgian style we see today.

has had many famous visitors – from ilaire Belloc, who admired the beer 1902, to Paul McCartney, who had Wonderful Christmas Time here in 979. And, of course, that beloved tar of 120 different stage roles, Sir aurence Olivier, who enjoyed his beer y the inglenook fireplace.

THE BASICS

istance: 3 miles: 4.75 km

radient: Level

everity: Easy

pprox time to walk: 80 minutes

tiles: Seven

laps: OS Landranger 198 (Brighton & Lewes); Explorer 122 (Brighton & Hove)

ath description: Mostly quiet lanes and tarmac drives; muddy section through farm

tart point: The Fountain Inn, Ashurst, BN44 3AP (Grid Ref. TQ 180161)

arking: Car park behind the Fountain Inn, by kind permission

og friendly: On a lead through the farms

ublic toilets: Only at the inn

earest food: The Fountain Inn

ASHURST WALK

1. From the car park return to the main road, cross carefully over and turn left. In just 25m turn right over a high stile following the footpath sign. Follow the path for 400m to the public road and turn right to the church of St James.

2. Follow Church Lane for 400m and where it takes a sharp right continue ahead along Ford Lane. Ignore the footpath to the right opposite 'Timbers' and in 300m reach Claylands Farm. At the far end of their large green metal barn turn right following the broad footpath.

3. In 250m, where the track swings left, turn right following the footpath fingerpost across an open field. Cross a plank bridge and stile over a small ditch and continue up the right-hand side of the next field aiming for the tallest tree ahead. Cross a stile beside a metal gate and follow the broad gravel track through farm buildings to the main road opposite Holly Tree Cottage.

4. Turn right along the road for 100m and, at the entrance to Merrion Farm on your left, cross carefully and walk down the broad farm track. This is a private road and permission has kindly been given by owner Alan Griffiths to walk down to the splendid Withyfield Cottage, where a public footpath joins the farm track. Follow the winding route of the track through the farm buildings to emerge through a metal gate into a small open field.

5. Cross the field and go over a double stile into the next field to walk beneath some splendid oak trees before passing through a metal kissing gate to a larger field. On reaching the four-armed fingerpost in the middle of this field continue straight ahead and walk up to the stile besides 'Eatons'.

6. Turn half right past the woodshed and continue to a gate at the far

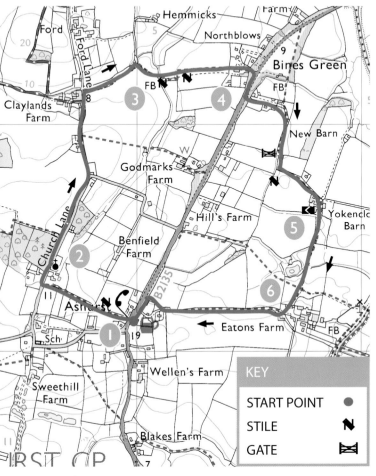

KEY

START POINT	●
STILE	➘
GATE	⋈

end of the wooden fencing. Turn right along the tarmac drive and follow this for 500m to reach a low building on your right and swing right to the main road where a left turn will bring you back, past Bloques Farmhouse, to the welcoming sight of the Fountain Inn.

ARDINGLY

THE PARISH OF ARDINGLY COVERS 50 SQUARE MILES WITH A POPULATION OF LESS THAN 2,000. MESOLITHIC FLINTS FOUND NEARBY SUGGEST THAT THIS AREA WAS INHABITED OVER 6,000 YEARS AGO.

The correct pronunciation of the name is ArdingLIE – derived from the Saxon word 'leah' meaning woodland clearing, and the family name Earda.

Ardingly College is one of three independent schools in Sussex, which are part of the Woodard Group. Nathaniel Woodard was a Church of England priest who was horrified by the chaos he saw in society. He believed that education was the only way of addressing this and founded his first school – Lancing College – in 1848. During his lifetime he founded ten further schools including Ardingly and Hurstpierpoint Colleges. His aim was to provide an education with a fundamental foundation based on 'sound principle and sound knowledge firmly grounded in the Christian faith'.

This college is built in the shape of an H and is dominated by the chapel and its tower. It is now fully co-educational with students ranging from pre-prep to university entrance level. A recent development at Ardingly has been the appointment of a Sculptor in Residence – Andrew Brown currently holds the post. As well as teaching he continues to create new sculptures – one, the life-size Good Samaritan, is directly on the walk. Private Eye editor Ian Hislop was educated at Ardingly College, where he started his satirical career, directing and appearing in revues, and became Head Prefect.

Ardingly Reservoir was constructed in the 1970s by the damming of two small brooks – the left-hand fork broadly follows the old course of the Shell Brook and the right-hand that of the Ardingly Brook. When full it holds an amazing 5,000 million litres of water. The area is now designated as a Local Nature Reserve. The main leisure activities are sailing, canoeing and windsurfing, mainly for educational purposes.

Continuing round to the small copse you can see beech, oak and ash trees; during the 1987 storm many were damaged and these have been left to provide shelter for fungi, lichens, mosses and insects. In spring and summer there are many wildflowers such as primroses, bluebells and common spotted orchids. There are two bird hides on the reservoir and this walk passes one – stop here a while to see what you can spot. If you're not sure about bird identification, there are information boards in the hide to help you.

Continuing along the main trail there is a rather scary giant stag beetle to the right. This was carved from a fallen tree trunk by South East Water's conservation ranger, Richard Dyer, who explained that since beetles like to live in dead wood it seemed appropriate to make one from it! Although there was a church here in the 12th century, much of the present building of St Peter's dates from about 1330, when this was the centre of the village. The west tower – the

THE BASICS

Distance: 3¼ miles: 5.2 km
Gradient: Easy descent but steep climb of 150 feet from the reservoir
Severity: Moderate because of climb
Approx time to walk: 110 minutes
Stiles: Three
Maps: OS Landranger 198: Explorer 135
Path description: Muddy in woodlands, otherwise good footpaths
Start point: Street Lane car park opposite the Ardingly Inn, RH17 6UA (Grid Ref. TQ 348294)
Parking: Free public car park
Dog friendly: Yes
Public toilets: At the northern end of the village and at the reservoir; also both inns
Nearest food: The Deli Café, Oak Inn or Ardingly Inn

only tower, as opposed to steeple, in the district – was added some 100 years later. The church boasts five old bells from the 17th and 18th centuries and a 'modern' treble added in 1911. Within the sanctuary there is an altar tomb and brass of Richard Wakehurst, who died in 1454. His daughter married Richard Culpeper and it was the Culpeper family who, in 1590, built the house we know as Wakehurst Place, which is now the country estate of the Royal Botanic Gardens and home of the Millennium Seed Bank.

The South of England Agricultural Society was formed in 1967 when they purchased this site from Sir Henry Price of Wakehurst Place. The first ever show was held that year over three days in June. The South of England Show now attracts over 90,000 visitors to Ardingly each year.

The Walk

1. From the car park walk past the Ardingly Inn and at the road junction ahead cross straight over College Road to the B2028 and follow the signs towards Lindfield. Follow the pavement downhill on the right hand side for 150m.

2. Turn right at the first public footpath sign on a drive between houses and in a few metres follow the path right then left to cross a high stile into open countryside. After a second stile cross a concrete drive, pass through a gate and continue downhill heading southwards across an open field.

3. At the corner of the wood ahead turn right on a crossing footpath and enter the wood on the far side of the field. The path exits this wood into a car park beside the hockey field, where pedestrian signs lead you to a road crossing.

4. Follow the drive into and through the college to where it drops steeply towards the 'pre-prep school'. Near the bottom of the hill, with a lake to your right continue ahead to Great Saucelands. Pass by the house and continue following the drive. Just before a gate turn left on a footpath into the woods and emerge over a stile into an open field.

5. Walk up to the far corner where there is a café with toilets and ice cream. After refreshments walk along the top of the dam and follow the Kingfisher Trail around the lakeside. After passing through a kissing gate there are some scary creatures in the trees to your right! Just 120m after the kissing gate turn right

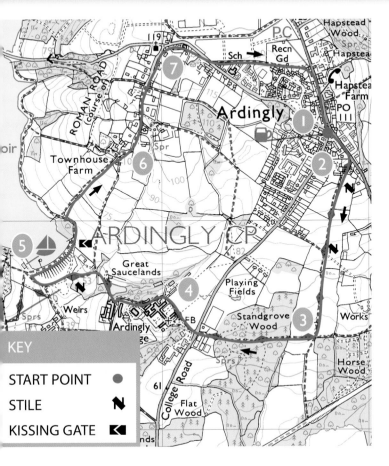

KEY

START POINT ●

STILE **N**

KISSING GATE ◄

through a gate following the footpath fingerpost heading uphill with the tree line to your right.

. At the top of the hill, besides an old barn, continue ahead on a farm track, which becomes a tarmac road and climbs gently to reach St. Peter's Church.

. At the road junction ahead turn right along Street Lane and follow this past the Church Centre. In a further 100m, just before the school sign, fork left on a tarmac footpath. Pass a children's play area and, just after the toilets, reach the main road. Turn right past the post office to return to the car park.

SINGLETON

The church in Singleton is mentioned in the Domesday Book of 1086. The tower is Saxon and is built of partially rendered rubble; the battlements were probably added later.

The church was originally dedicated to St Mary, but due to an error in the 19th century it was attributed to St John Evangelist until 1979, when it once again became St Mary's.

The walk follows a wide valley formed by the River Lavant — a celtic river-name meaning 'gliding one'. This rises in a pond in the village of East Dean to the east and flows through Chichester to the harbour. It is a winterbourne, meaning that traditionally it flows mostly in winter. Over a few very dry years the Lavant virtually disappeared but in recent wet years it has caused major floods in Singleton and Chichester — leading one newspaper to call it 'the little river that roared'.

St Roche's Hill, better known as The Trundle, was occupied in palaeolithic times. It was later a neolithic 'causewayed camp' and then an Iron Age hill fort, the name The Trundle coming from an Old English word for circle.

St Roche is the patron saint of healing. Born in 1295 he worked with plague sufferers and there was once a chapel dedicated to him on top of the hill. His saint's day is on 16th August and every year a service takes place on the chapel site.

Levin Down nature reserve is managed by the Sussex Wildlife Trust and is a Site of Special Scientific Interest (SSSI). The reason that Levin is such an important site for wildlife is suggested in its name, which is derived from 'leave-alone hill' — the land has never been intensively farmed. The down is the largest area of chalk heath in Sussex and is a rare and important habitat. It is still a managed landscape, including scrub clearance and grazing to maintain the right balance of plants. An information sheet can be found at www.sussexwildlifetrust.org.uk.

The impressive finger post at Hunters Gate commemorates the most famous day in the history of the Charlton Hunt – the 'Grand Chase'. The hounds ran continuously from 8 in the morning to 6 at night. The Duke of Richmond was so pleased to have ridden the whole day that he sent his servants out with a cartwheel to check the distance – 57 miles. The current post replaced an older one from the 1970s when a hunt was still going strong in this area. It provided directions for riders who had lost their way.

The New Lipchis Way is a 39 mile trail from Liphook to East Head created by the authors of this book. A leaflet is available from www.newlipchisway.co.uk.

The distinctive white building of Goodwood Racecourse dates from 1979, although further stands have been added since. Horse racing has taken place here since 1801 when the third Duke of Richmond introduced racing for the benefit of officers of the Sussex Militia of which he was Colonel. Nineteen racing events a year are now held here including the sparkling 'Glorious Goodwood' – a sporting highlight in the social calendar.

THE BASICS

Distance: 3¼ miles: 5.2 km
Gradient: Two easy ascents and one slightly steeper descent
Severity: Moderate
Approx time to walk: 90 minutes
Stiles: One
Maps: OS Landranger 197 (Chichester & the South Downs); Explorer 120 (Chichester)
Path description: Mostly grassy tracks; one section of narrow path on Levin Down
Start point: The Partridge Inn, Singleton, PO18 0EY (Grid Ref. SU 877131)
Parking: Roadside parking near the Partridge Inn
Dog friendly: Cattle and sheep throughout the walk
Public toilets: Only at the inn
Nearest food: Teashop or Partridge Inn in Singleton

SINGLETON WALK

1. With your back to the pub entrance turn left to walk along the road heading eastwards for just 50m and at Easter Cottage turn right towards the church.

2. In front of the church turn left to walk past the children's play area and through 'The Leys' to follow a yellow footpath arrow into a large open field and walk straight ahead for 15 minutes to reach a public road.

3. Turn left and at the road junction turn left again for just 75m to reach a kissing gate on the right. Walk through this and follow the footpath uphill to a gate where there is a bench with fine views of the Lavant Valley and the two aerials atop 'The Trundle' opposite.

4. Pass immediately through a second gate and turn half right past the information board. A further gate leads to a fork in the path; keep left going more steeply uphill. This well-trodden path leads around the open hillside of Levin Down with its profusion of wildflowers, and eventually enters a wooded area where a stile and a gate lead out onto open downland. Here turn right heading downhill to the lower right hand corner of the field.

5. Pass briefly through a small wood to emerge onto a wide crossing bridleway and turn left uphill to reach Hunters Gate with its splendid fingerpost. Follow the arm pointing towards Singleton, through a metal gate, along a bridleway. The route to follow is towards the far corner of the tree line on your right over the western flank of Levin Down.

6. As you reach the highest point of the walk join a wire fence on your right and descend gently through a gate with fine views of Goodwood Racecourse in the distance. The bridleway curves slowly right around the hillside and goes straight over a crossing footpath following the 'New Lipchis Way' towards a clump of trees.

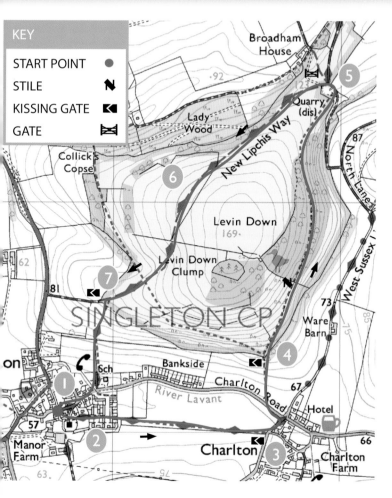

KEY

START POINT	●
STILE	N
KISSING GATE	◄
GATE	✕

7. On reaching the first tree on your right, take the left fork in the track leading down to a kissing gate and then almost immediately go through a second gate with views of the village directly below. Follow the clear path quite steeply downhill to pass beside the primary school to exit onto the public road and turn right. At the fork in the road, the tearooms are to your right and the inn to your left.

BURPHAM

The name of this pretty village derives from two Old English words. 'ham' and 'burgh', which also – in that order – spell the name of a much larger town in Germany!

It simply means 'fortified settlement' and refers to the original defensive earthworks built around AD 900 to guard against Viking raiders plundering their way up the valley. You'll encounter the earthworks of the fort at the end of the walk as you climb up from Splash Farm.

The village originally grew up within the Saxon fort but shifted itself to the northern entrance by the early Norman period where the 11th-century church was constructed. An unusual feature worth looking for in the chancel of St Mary's Church is the lepers' window. The low window allowed lepers from the nearby colony, at what is now Lee Farm, to view the service without coming into contact with others. Such was our ignorance and fear of leprosy. The track you will walk along Coombe Lane is the route they took to and from church and is known as the Lepers Way.

For hundreds of years the River Arun provided a means of communication for the village but, with the cutting of a new river channel by the railway company in the 1860s the Burpham Loop, as it was known, became a backwater and the village wharf closed in 1887.

This walk is mostly through delightfully quiet and remote countryside, much of which was acquired by the Norfolk Estate at the end of the 18th century. The unspoilt nature of the area has attracted its fair share of writers and artists, the most well known being perhaps John Cooper Powys, Mervyn Peake and 'beekeeper' Tickner Edwardes, who features in our Arun Valley walk.

The inn at the end of the walk was for many years called the George and Dragon. The name was shortened in 2013 when it was acquired by a group of 'locals' who now manage it very much as a communal centre with a small shop selling local produce

THE BASICS

Distance: 3½ miles: 5.5 km

Gradient: Short, easy ascent and a flight of steps; steeper road section downhill

Severity: Easy/moderate

Approx time to walk: 100 minutes

Stiles: Six

Maps: OS Landranger 197 (Chichester & the South Downs); Explorer 121 (Arundel & Pulborough)

Path description: Wide bostal (downland path) and grassy tracks with some quiet country lanes

Start point: The George Inn, Burpham, BN18 9RR (Grid Ref. TQ 039089)

Parking: Free public car park behind the George Inn

Dog friendly: Sheep on the downland section

Public toilets: Only at the inn

Nearest food: The George Inn, Burpham

BURPHAM WALK

1. From the car park walk back towards the George Inn and turn right. Keep left at the first fork in the road and continue ahead past Burpham Country House Hotel to a road junction. Turn right downhill and in 75m take the first bridleway left along Coombe Lane.

2. Walk past a house and water station to reach a wooden gate and soon afterwards turn right following the yellow footpath sign on a grassy path heading upwards to the horizon. Near the top of this rise cross a stile besides a gate and continue straight ahead to join a much broader crossing path and turn right.

3. As you pass a large clump of trees on your left the path becomes grassy and continues ahead with fine views of the Isle of Wight in the distance. After passing through a metal gate begin descending gently downhill as Arundel Castle comes into view further down the valley. On reaching the next junction of paths cross a stile and turn half right heading more steeply downhill. The path immediately swings left and crosses two more stiles before reaching the public road.

4. Turn left and in just 50m take the first road right heading steeply downhill towards Splash Farm. Cross the ford on the raised path and take the path ahead going up wooden steps on the side of the hill through the trees. At the top cross two more stiles across an open field and turn right past the children's playground to the car park behind the George Inn.

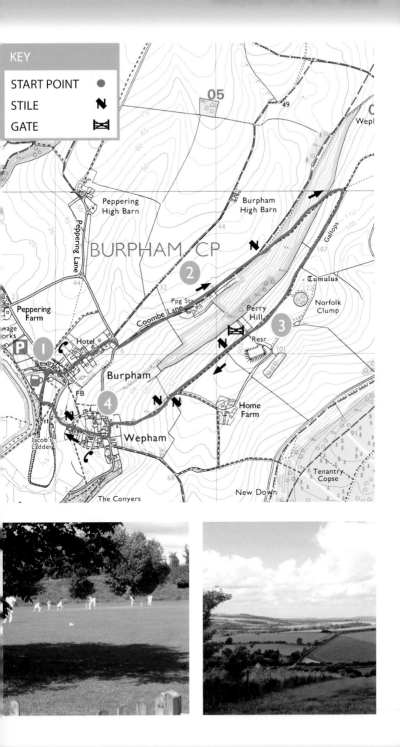

KEY

START POINT ●

STILE

GATE

05

49

Weph

Peppering High Barn

Burpham High Barn

Gallops

BURPHAM CP

Peppering Lane

44

107

110
105

Tumulus

Norfolk Clump

2

Ppg Sta

Coombe Lane

Perry Hill

3

Resr

Peppering Farm

101

wage orks

P

Hotel

Burpham

FB

Home Farm

4

Wepham

Jacob's Ladder

Tenantry Copse

New Down

The Conyers

WARNINGLID

THE PICTURESQUE VILLAGE OF WARNINGLID IS SITUATED ON A HILL IN THE HIGH WEALD AREA OF OUTSTANDING NATURAL BEAUTY (AONB). THE HIGH WEALD HAS A COMPLEX GEOLOGY OF CLAYS AND SANDSTONES CREATING A ROLLING LANDSCAPE OF RIDGES AND VALLEYS

This is one of the most densely wooded areas in England. There are areas of ancient woodland and more recent plantations mixed with a patchwork of small fields separated by hedgerows and smaller chunks of woodland. As an AONB the area enjoys a high level of protection from modern development and retains many traditional and historic features.

The village itself is dominated by The Street, running south from the pub. The variety of ages and styles of building, with the predominant use of traditional building materials, make this an attractive road, full of character. Many of these buildings are listed and this was one of the first conservation areas designated in Sussex, giving protection from the worst excesses of modern times. The village has won the 'Best Kept Village' competition three times in the last 25 years and been runner-up six times.

The name Warninglid is believed to come from two words meaning 'Werna's Path'. The village sign was put up in the late 1970s by the Warninglid Residents Society and shows Werna, a Saxon warrior with sword and shield standing in a leafy glade.

For a while this walk follows the High Weald Landscape Trail. This is a 95-mile (155 km) waymarked route that wanders across, as the name suggests, the High Weald from Horsham in West Sussex to Rye on the East Sussex coast.

Although now largely agricultural, this was once a busy industrial landscape. Iron making was important in the High Weald from pre-Roman times and during the Middle Ages iron production was at its peak. The Weald is rich in iron ore and the necessary fuel to process it. Charcoal from the local woodland was used for the furnaces and later water power – both of which are plentiful in the area. In the 16th century the Weald was well placed to serve the growing demand for iron from London and coastal towns; in particular there was a demand to make armaments for the army, navy and coastal fortifications.

The early Industrial Revolution saw the end of large-scale iron production in the Weald as coal became the main source of power and improved transport opened up other areas in Britain. The iron industry has left its mark on the Weald, including landscape features such as large furnace ponds with dams, mill races, leats and overflow channels. Now a peaceful rural landscape, these are havens for wildlife and sources of leisure activities such as fishing, walking and birdwatching.

The Weald has a network of roads, lanes, footpaths and tracks, many of which have been used for over a thousand years. These linked the many dispersed farms, hamlets and small villages. Others were traditionally 'drover ways', routes taken by farmers and

THE BASICS

Distance: 3½ miles: 5.6 km

Gradient: Slow descent to the lake and gentle climb back up

Severity: Moderate

Approx time to walk: 90 minutes

Stiles: Four

Maps: OS Landranger 198 (Brighton & Lewes); Explorer 134 (Crawley & Horsham)

Path description: Mainly open fields with a short section of woodland and narrow lakeside path; quiet country lane at the end

Start point: The Half Moon Inn, Warninglid, RH17 5TR (Grid Ref. TQ 250261)

Parking: The inn car park (by kind permission)

Dog friendly: Yes

Public toilets: Only at the inn

Nearest food: The Half Moon, Warninglid

herders moving their livestock around the county. Some were routes to and from markets, used at a time when animals were taken on foot rather than in the mass transportation of today. Others run north–south, marking the routes by which stock was moved between woodland and downland on a seasonal basis – known as 'transhumance'.

It seems that the Half Moon has no real history of haunting, although a previous landlord of Irish descent was known to have a number of stories ready to tell any American visitors who asked. He would also claim to have been the only person ever to unite the whole village, saying: 'They all joined together in opposition when I threatened to close the pub!' Thankfully under today's owners it is still open and thriving.

The Walk

1. Turn left out of the car park and walk down The Street for 150m and immediately after Herring Cottages turn left following the footpath fingerpost to soon cross a stile and enter open countryside. After another stile and a couple of kissing gates reach a public road; here turn left and then right over a plank bridge and head diagonally across the next field.

2. Cross another plank bridge, after which three metal gates lead to a crossing footpath. Turn left on the farm track past the stables to reach the main road and turn left along the grass verge. After just 100m cross the road carefully to the footpath fingerpost on the other side and turn right over a stile into a large field.

3. Enter the woodland ahead with its splendid beech trees and follow the winding path downwards through the trees. (At a sharp dip in the path look to your right to spot a secret fairy glen.) Exit the woods over a plank bridge and continue downhill over the next open field. Take care as you reach the trees on your right; the path continues straight ahead at this point, veering away from the tree line to pass between two ponds and reach a broad farm track. Pass through farm buildings and drop more steeply down to reach the lakeside.

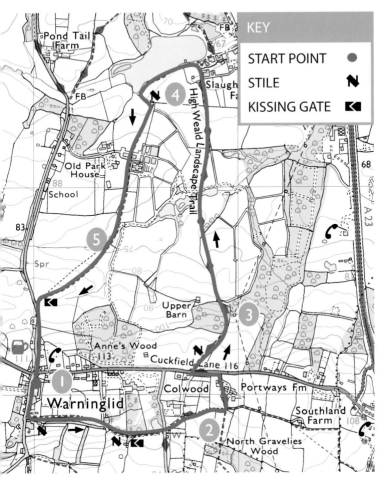

KEY

START POINT ●

STILE N

KISSING GATE ◄

4. Turn left along the lakeside beside Slaugham Place Farm. Nearing the end of the lake the path goes left over a stile and after crossing a small ditch starts to climb gently towards farm buildings. Pass behind the large barn to walk beside the paddocks, and at the end of these reach a fingerpost indicating that the path goes half right through a large gap in the hedge line and not along the more obvious farm drive.

5. Follow the hedge to your right for 100m then turn half left, going uphill across the middle of this open field on a well-trodden path. The path eventually leaves the field through a kissing gate onto the public road where a left turn along the pavement will return you to the Half Moon.

WEST ITCHENOR

Itchenor takes its name from a Saxon chieftain, Icca, who settled in the district after the Romans left. The village is still called West Itchenor despite East Itchenor disappearing centuries ago.

The village of Bosham can be seen across the harbour. It is said that this is where King Canute unsuccessfully tried to stop the tide, afterwards saying: 'Let all the world know that the power of kings is empty and worthless and there is no king worthy of the name save Him by whose will heaven and earth and sea obey eternal laws.'

The church was built in the 12th century and has been considerably altered over time. I contains some interesting modern stained glass windows. St Nicholas is, appropriately, the patron saint of seafarers and also of children.

Itchenor Park House was built in the late 18th century for the third Duke of Richmond as a yachting lodge. His coat of arms can be seen on the farm building to the right of the path It is said that the house was built for the Duke's mistress, Madame de Cambis. After his death in 1806 their daughter inherited a life interest in Itchenor Park and lived there with her husband.

Chichester Harbour is very important environmentally and has many national and international designations for landscape and nature conservation, which help protec it. These include: Area of Outstanding Natural Beauty (AONB), Site of Special Scientific Interest (SSSI), Special Area of Conservation (SAC) and Special Protection Area (SPA) and Ramsar Wetland of International Importance. It is also a major area for recreation and leisure and is commercially important for agriculture, fishing, boatyards and tourism. This presents something of a challenge for all those involved in its management.

The Chichester Harbour Conservancy was established in 1971 to 'conserve, maintain and improve' the harbour and the immediately surrounding area for recreation, leisure, conservation and natural beauty. Their website www.conservancy.co.uk provides a wealth of information about the harbour or pick up one of their many publications at their offices on the harbour edge in Itchenor.

The rich range of harbour habitats includes the deep water channel, mudflats, shingle banks, saltmarsh, grazing marsh, sand dunes and ancient woodland. Together they provide homes for a huge range of plants, birds and animals. More than 55,000 birds live on or visit the harbour each year. The mud is a very rich source of food. Some birds use their long beaks to find

worms and small shellfish down in the mud, others pick up food from the surface or find it under stones and seaweed. Some are vegetarian, eating plants growing on the mud while fish-eaters either dive or fish in the shallows. The Conservancy website gives details of all these different birds.

Over 10,000 boats use the harbour, now mostly for leisure. Small warships were built at Itchenor for centuries and boat building remains an important activity. The boatyard towards the end of the walk is famous for wooden boat building. It was a family business and is now owned by an independent company. Only members of Itchenor Sailing Club are allowed to become shareholders.

Boat trips around the harbour leave the quay at Itchenor four times daily during the high season and are an excellent and enjoyable way to learn more about the area.

THE BASICS

Distance: 4 miles: 6.4 km

Gradient: A flat coastal walk

Severity: Easy

Approx time to walk: 110 minutes

Stiles: One

Maps: OS Landranger 197 (Chichester & the South Downs); Explorer 120 (Chichester)

Path description: Narrow waterside paths with good inland tracks

Start point: The car park in West Itchenor, PO20 7AH (Grid Ref. SU 798012)

Parking: Pay & display car park just before the Ship Inn

Dog friendly: Yes

Public toilets: By the Harbour Office and at the inn

Nearest food: The Ship Inn, Itchenor

WEST ITCHENOR WALK

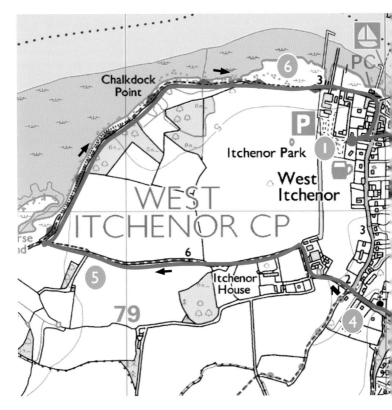

1. From the car park walk back towards the main road (The Street) and turn left. In just 40m, opposite the Ship Inn, turn right following the footpath fingerpost down a drive to reach the waterfront. Here turn right on a narrower path along the water's edge. You are following the New Lipchis Way.

2. After five minutes or so the path leaves the harbour side to reach a tarmac drive where a left turn leads down a millionaire's row of lovely houses. At the end of this avenue turn right to pass through a gate and walk along the edge of a small wood. On leaving the trees cross an open field and at the far side, on reaching a hedgerow, turn sharp right in front of the hedge.

3. The path continues westward across more open country and on reaching a large

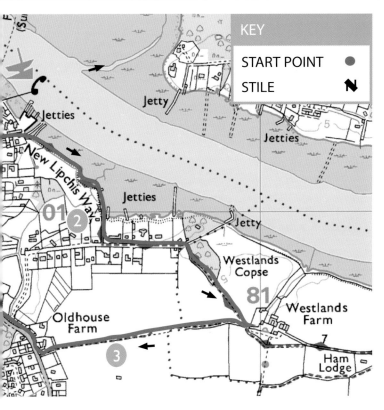

concrete barn narrows onto a gravel track between fences to cross a small footbridge and reach the public road. Turn right along the grass verge and in 50m cross carefully over to a wider verge on the other side and continue ahead to the church of St Nicholas.

. After visiting the church carry on over the brow of the hill to where the road makes a sharp right. Here continue straight ahead following a tarmac drive into Itchenor Park House and Farm. In 150m, in front of a gate, turn right along a flint wall following the 'All Farm Traffic' sign. The footpath goes through a gap in the wall and then

crosses a stile onto a concrete track. Turn left with a large open field to your right.

5. The concrete track eventually gives way to a grassy track, which, after passing through two pinch-points, reaches the harbour shoreline once more. Turn right and as you walk this pretty path through the trees take care of the roots beneath your feet.

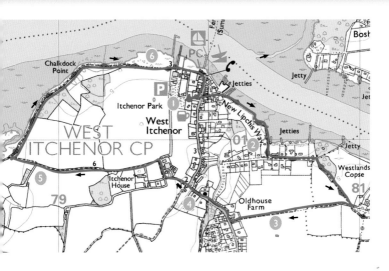

After leaving the trees the track becomes a tarmac surface and reaches a large boatyard. Go carefully straight across the yard to a path between tall hedges which shortly leads to the Chichester Harbour Conservancy office where there are toilets and 90-minute boat trips available. From here a right turn will return you along The Street to the Ship Inn and the car park.

STOUGHTON

OUR WALK STARTS IN THE PRETTY VILLAGE OF STOUGHTON, CLIMBING STEADILY UP TO THE DOWNS WITH BEAUTIFUL VIEWS IN ALL DIRECTIONS. ALONG ONE SIDE OF THE VILLAGE GREEN RUNS THE RIVER EMS.

This rises as a spring just to the east of the village and flows into Chichester Harbour at Emsworth. As a chalk stream it is ecologically important, providing homes for, amongst others, the water vole. Further towards Emsworth it was diverted at various points to power water mills and it has long been a source of water for the Portsmouth area.

Just to the north of the green is the church of St Mary, which is worth a visit whether before or after the walk. It has been described as 'plain outside but impressively rich inside'. This church was mentioned in the Domesday Book of 1086 and is Saxon in origin although the building we see now has been greatly changed over the centuries.

The first part of the walk follows a short section of the Monarch's Way. This is a 615 mile (990 km) waymarked trail following as closely as possible the route taken by Charles II as he escaped after defeat at the Battle of Worcester in 1651.

The name Stoughton is Old English for a farmstead at an outlying hamlet, suggesting remoteness and this is still the case, with just one quiet road passing through. It is easy to imagine Charles and his friends thundering by on their horses as they evaded the Parliamentarian troops following them. He eventually found a ship to take him to France from Shoreham-by-Sea.

Our walk passes through the edge of Kingley Vale. Some of the oldest and finest yew trees in Europe grow here and a few are amongst the oldest living things in Britain. It is not known exactly how o hese trees are. Some say the men of Chichester planted them as early as AD 849 in nemory of Viking warriors killed in battle. Others say they were planted in the Middle Ages to make longbows.

The whole area is rich in prehistoric remains. At the highest point on the walk are the remains of burial barrows, known as the Devil's Humps. Although it has been

established that these date from the Bronze Age, they are sometimes called the 'King's Graves' and it is said that the leaders of the Vikings mentioned above were buried in them.

The immense yew trees grow in many weird shapes and are contorted by age. There are many stories about these woods and the barrows. Ghosts are believed to haunt them and it is said that the trees come alive and move around at night. There is a tale that if you run round the barrows seven times the devil will appear.

The Tansley Stone is a monument to the 20th-century ecologist Sir Arthur Tansley. A plaque is

THE BASICS

Distance: 4 miles: 6.4 km
Gradient: Steady climb of over 500 feet to splendid views
Severity: Challenging
Approx time to walk: 115 minutes
Stiles: None
Maps: OS Landranger 197 (Chichester & the South Downs); Explorer 120 (Chichester)
Path description: Broad tracks, generally good surface
Start point: The village green, Stoughton, PO18 9JQ (Grid Ref. SU 802114)
Parking: Disused bus stop beside the village green
Dog friendly: Yes
Public toilets: Only at the inn
Nearest food: The Hare and Hounds, Stoughton

attached to a sarsen stone from where he used to admire the view of Kingley Vale. He was very important in campaigning for nature conservation and chaired the committee that recommended the formation of the Nature Conservancy (now Natural England). This led to the establishment of National Nature Reserves – a designation now afforded to Kingley Vale. They are some of the most important sites of nature conservation in Britain. To find out more about them visit www.naturalengland.org.uk.

Towards the end of the walk is a memorial to a Polish pilot, Bolesław Własnowolski. He was based at Tangmere and on 1 November 1940 was shot down in his Hurricane plane at the age of just 23. He was on patrol intercepting incoming Luftwaffe bombers and had shot down at least five enemy planes in the months before his death.

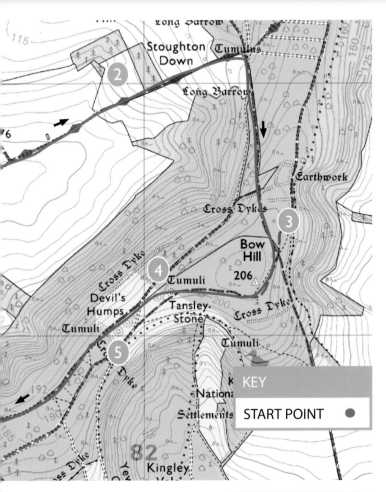

KEY

START POINT ●

THE WALK

1. Walk northwards through the village, past the Hare and Hounds, and in front of a lovely L-shaped house called 'Old Bartons' turn right following the yellow public footpath sign up a concrete drive, which is also the Monarch's Way. The path immediately swings left and becomes a rough, broad track. Continue straight ahead as this footpath becomes a bridleway and starts to climb more steeply.

2. The path narrows and shortly levels off besides a bench. In a further 50m, at a T-junction, turn right on a broad bridleway with a tall tree line to your left. Take care now – in just a further 50m your route goes left away from the main track on a narrower bridleway into the trees. This is a long, sometimes steepish climb to the top of the downs.

3. Follow the path over the top of the downs and start to descend slowly. Just as the views open out spectacularly to the south-east, turn right on a crossing bridleway. Follow this almost level track past the old trig point with occasional views to the south coast on your left, before opening out to the amazing sight of the Devil's Humps.

4. Just at this point deviate a little to your right and you will come across the Tansley Stone from where you can follow a well-worn path straight across the tops of the humps – which is a much more fun way to cross this 'access land'.

5. From the top of the last, most southerly, hump turn right heading north-west and you will immediately reach a broad bridleway. Turn left and follow this through the trees as it begins to descend gently. At the end of the wood reach a T-junction of paths and turn right.

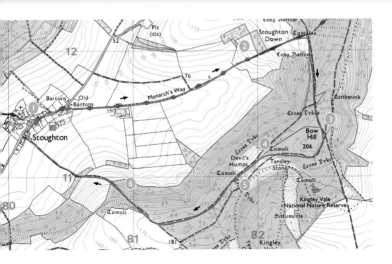

. The path steepens a little and re-enters woodland before finally opening out with fine views of the village and valley below. It passes a memorial to a Polish pilot before emerging onto the main road where a right turn will return you to the village green and the inn.

SLINDON

THE FORGE IN SLINDON OPENED IN 2012 THROUGH
COMMUNITY EFFORT AND CO-OPERATION. AS THE NAME
SUGGESTS THE BUILDING WAS ORIGINALLY THE VILLAGE
BLACKSMITH AND THERE ARE MANY REMINDERS OF THIS.

The shop sells a wide range of products and
the café provides lovely cakes and meals.
The building also acts as a local information
point, including an interactive touch-screen
installed by the National Trust.

Many villages in Sussex claim to be the 'cradle of cricket' and there is no doubt that
Slindon has a very old cricket club. The distinctive village sign commemorates this. It
was put up to mark the millennium by the Slindon Pudding Club, a group of villagers
who raise money to help needy members of the community and fund village initiatives.
Slindon produced some great 18th-century cricketers. Richard Newland was a fine left-
handed batsman and bowler. In the 1740s, an all-England team was beaten by 'poor
little Slyndon . . . in almost one innings'.

In the time of Queen Elizabeth I it was forbidden to worship as a Roman Catholic. As
far back as then the family living in Slindon House were Catholic and their successors
remained so until emancipation in 1829. They would worship in secret and Slindon House
was one place where a chapel existed. A 'priest's hole' was found here with its secret
passage allowing the priest to escape through the cellars. The death penalty for being a
Catholic priest was removed in the 1680s, but those who refused to give up Catholicism
were subject to heavy fines and taxes. Many families converted to Protestantism and
Slindon was one of the few places in Sussex where tiny congregations of Catholics
continued.

The Catholic church of St Richard was built in the
1860s. Anne, Countess of Newburgh, who lived in
Slindon House, was a devout Catholic and endowed
both this church and one in Chichester – also
dedicated to St Richard.

The National Trust now owns and manages the
3,500-acre Slindon Estate. It was bequeathed to
them in the 1950s with the condition that 'the whole
be maintained as far as possible as a Sussex estate

They also own around two-thirds of the houses in the village as well as Slindon House. When the National Trust surveyor visited the estate in 1944 he described the park and estate as 'a dream of beauty but . . . the house is a travesty'. Although originally an Elizabethan house, it has been vastly altered, resulting in the flint building we see today. Slindon House is now a college – an independent day and boarding school offering specialist learning support to boys aged 8 to 16.

The Countess of Newburgh had Nore Folly built around 1814. She asked an unemployed bricklayer, Samuel Refoy, if he could build her a copy of an arch shown in a print brought back from Italy. She was so pleased with the result that he was made estate bricklayer at Slindon House. The folly was later used by the countess for picnics and shooting parties.

The walk passes through some attractive woodland. The National Trust actively manages these woods by thinning the trees to let more light through for wildflowers and other woodland plants to grow. They also deliberately leave piles of brush and logs to provide a rich habitat for wildlife.

Slindon is famous for its pumpkin display. Over 40 years ago Ralph Upton started growing pumpkins here and each autumn an amazing display is created using a vast number of different-coloured and shaped pumpkins. Ralph died in 2009 at the age of 87 but the tradition has continued, thanks to his son Robin.

THE BASICS

Distance: 4½ miles: 7.2 km

Gradient: Steady climb all the way to the folly; smaller hills thereafter

Severity: Moderate

Approx time to walk: 120 minutes

Stiles: None

Maps: OS Landranger 197 (Chichester & the South Downs); Explorer 121 (Arundel & Pulborough)

Path description: Good farm tracks and quiet country lanes

Start point: The Forge Café and Shop, Reynolds Lane, Slindon BN18 0QT (Grid Ref. SU 966079)

Parking: Free public car park beside the café

Dog friendly: Yes

Public toilets: In the café/shop

Nearest food: The Forge Café, Slindon or the Spur Inn on the A29

SLINDON WALK

1. From the car park walk past the café up towards the centre of the village and on passing the village sign, continue to your right up School Hill. In 200m, at the next road junction, turn left into Church Hill and walk past the village pond and St Mary's Church to a T-junction at the top of the hill.

2. Turn left past the Catholic church and just after the entrance to Slindon College, beside the speed de-restriction sign, turn right down an unmarked but clear path between the trees (not the bridleway through the gate). At the bottom continue ahead on the tarmac lane for just 100m then turn left on a broad farm track following the yellow footpath sign.

3. After 600m, before reaching a stone barn on the left, look for a fingerpost indicating a footpath going uphill to the right. Follow this grassy track almost to the top of the hill, where a sharp left turn brings you to the folly. Leave here on the farm track over the brow of the hill to pass through a metal gate onto a pleasant forest ride.

4. In 400m reach a T-junction and turn right on the descending bridleway. In a further 75m, where the path forks, keep right, heading more steeply downhill to reach a crossing bridleway at the bottom of the hill and turn right. At the edge of the wood reach a four-armed fingerpost and turn right again on the crossing bridleway. Soon reach a tarmac road and continue ahead, slightly to the right.

5. Take care now – in 250m fork left into the trees, away from the road, following a blue bridleway sign. Follow this through the woods then uphill across an open field and at the T-junction at the top of the hill turn right. There follow two close forks in the bridleway; at the first keep right; at the second keep left. You should now be climbing slightly through the trees.

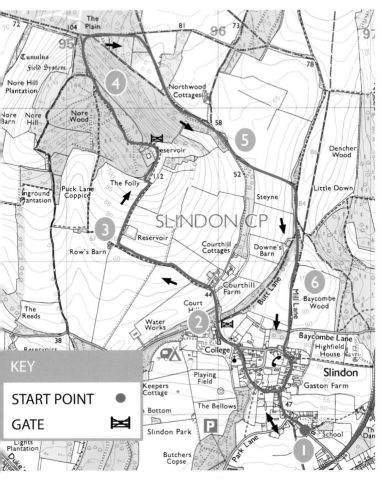

KEY

START POINT ●

GATE ⌖

6. Follow the track over the rise and, as the rooftops of Slindon come into view, drop down to join the public road which is Mill Lane. Continue straight ahead to the T-junction in the village and turn left. Follow the road as it swings right down School Hill and becomes Reynolds Lane with the welcoming sight of the Forge Café.

WASHINGTON

WASHINGTON IS DERIVED FROM OLD ENGLISH, MEANING 'THE ESTATE OF THE FAMILY OR FOLLOWERS OF A MAN CALLED WASSA' AND WAS FIRST RECORDED IN AD 957. THE VILLAGE GREW UP AT THE CROSSING OF TWO MAIN ROUTES.

One followed an east - west ridge and the other ran north - south between London and Worthing.

In the late 19th century there were many stores and businesses serving the local population, in the 1920s three tearooms catered for increasing numbers of visitors arising from the growth of tourism by motor car. Sadly they have all long since closed. Washington is another village in Sussex that has, however, benefitted from local community action and it now has a small shop beside the pub and teas are served at weekends in the village hall.

The memorial at the entrance to Sullington churchyard commemorates four local men who died in action during the First World War and the crew of submarine E24, which was sunk by a mine off Heligoland in March 1916. Lt. Cdr. Napier, captain of the E24, was a Sullington man.

Many ancient paths cross the downs here. Bostal is a Sussex name for a narrow, winding track, usually climbing the steep north-facing escarpment. Just south of here were many flint mines. These are believed by many to be the last home of fairies in England.

At the top of the downs the walk follows a section of the South Downs Way, a 100-mile national trail from Winchester to Eastbourne. This broadly follows the ancient track along the top, but is not a rigidly fixed route. This walk follows a diverted section back down into Washington, crossing the busy A24 on a farm bridge. The original route leads to a dangerous crossing of the main road.

On the downs beyond the A24 can be seen the distinctive Chanctonbury Ring. It was an Iron Age hill fort and the remains of a Roman temple have been found here. The ring is visible for many miles and beacons were placed here to warn of possible invasions during the time of the Spanish Armada and the Napoleonic Wars.

Charles Goring planted the beech trees around the ring in 1760. There was a public outcry, as local people feared the line of the beautiful downs would be spoilt for future generations. However, the trees have become a landmark and their devastation in the storm of 1987 was greatly regretted. They are now beginning to recover.

The pub was originally called the Washington Inn and was built as a coaching inn on the

London to Worthing road. It was made famous in Hilaire Belloc's book 'The Four Men' by the claim: 'the swipes they take in at the Washington Inn, is the very best beer I know.' This beer was brewed at Mitchell's Brewery in Steyning and such high praise did not do them much good as it closed in 1914. The change of name to the Frankland Arms celebrates William Frankland, a wealthy East Indian Company merchant, adventurer and collector of unusual machinery who lived in a large house just south of the village.

THE BASICS

Distance: 4½ miles: 7.2 km

Gradient: One long, easy ascent and one slightly steeper descent

Severity: Moderate

Approx time to walk: 120 minutes

Stiles: None

Maps: OS Landrangers 197 (Chichester & the South Downs) and 198 (Brighton & Lewes); Explorer 121 (Arundel & Pulborough)

Path description: Mostly broad bostal tracks; one muddy section in wet weather

Start point: Frankland Arms Inn, Washington RH20 4AL (Grid Ref. TQ 122129)

Parking: Unrestricted roadside parking

Dog friendly: Cattle and sheep on the downland section

Public toilets: Only at the inn

Nearest food: The Frankland Arms, Washington

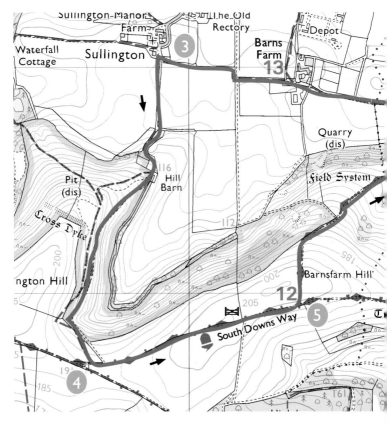

1. With your back to the inn turn right and walk along the road for 200m, then turn right into 'The Street'. After passing St Mary's Church cross the busy A24 on the road bridge and at the next fork keep right. In just 100m, on reaching the first house, turn left into the trees and then almost immediately right following a blue bridleway sign.

2. Follow this path left then right as it emerges into open fields with fine views now o the South Downs ahead to your left. The path goes around Barns Farm, at the fa side of which you must turn left to continue westwards on a more confined pat between trees. At the end of this tree line take care as you cross the gallops the

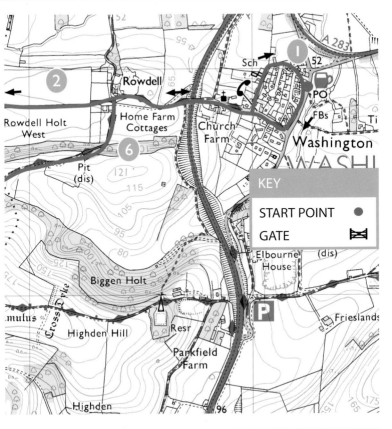

KEY

START POINT   ●

GATE   ⛩

continue in the same direction along the side of an open field to reach Sullington Manor Farm.

3. Turn right to visit the lovely church, in this peaceful and picturesque setting. Now retrace your steps to where you entered the farmyard and head directly south towards the downs on a broad track. This briefly becomes concreted and climbs quite steeply before passing a low farm building, after which the gradient eases into a typical downland bostal.

4. At the crest of the downs, just east of a hay barn, meet the crossing South Downs Way national trail and turn left to follow it. After crossing the brow of the next hill the trail begins its slow descent back towards Washington and soon passes through a metal gate. Just 250m after this gate take care to look for a turning to the left off the main trail following the 'alternative route avoiding the A24'.

5. Turn left here and initially climb over a rise and pass a clump of bushes before beginning a long curving descent north-eastwards (take care that you are following the bridleway and not a wide farm track as you pass the bushes).

6. Near the foot of the downs the path enters trees and turns north to pass beside 'The Old Pump House' and reach a crossroad of tracks. Continue ahead into the trees and in just 25m, at the T-junction, turn right to retrace the steps of your outbound route. After again passing St Mary's Church take the first road left and walk quite steeply down School Lane past the village hall and playing fields to emerge beside the garden of the Frankland Arms.

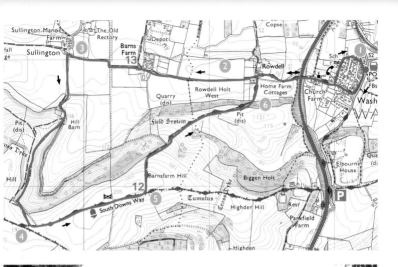

HURSTPIERPOINT

THE NAME HURSTPIERPOINT COMES FROM AN OLD ENGLISH WORD 'HERST' MEANING A WOODED HILL AND PIERRE PONT, THE FAMILY NAME OF THE NORMAN BARON WHO WAS GIVEN LANDS HERE AFTER THE NORMAN CONQUEST.

The village sign is a copy of the effigy of Simon de Pierre Pont found in the church. He was the last member of that family to live here and died in 1343.

The church building on the bend in St George's Lane was built in 1852 by Colonel Charles Hannington. He had a serious disagreement with the local rector supposedly telling him 'not to come the High Priest over me!' The argument was resolved in 1867 and the chapel became part of the Church of England. It has very recently been converted into a striking private house.

Coldharbour is a common name in Sussex and there are many debates as to its meaning. One likely meaning is a place of sanctuary or shelter, perhaps for those travelling with their own bedding and provisions.

The alpacas are huacaya. They come from the high Andes and were domesticated by the Incas. Alpacas are closely related to llamas but are much smaller and are bred for their fleece while llamas are generally used as pack animals. Alpaca wool is smoother and less prickly than sheep's; it contains no lanolin and is good for those allergic to other types of wool. Sheep also graze the Danny estate and their spring lambs are protected from foxes by two llamas. Alpacas were found not to be good guards but the llamas have successfully earned their keep.

The name Danny is a corruption of the Saxon Danehithe, meaning 'valley and haven'. There has been a house on this site since the 13th century. Originally a hunting lodge, the current house was built during the reign of Queen Elizabeth I by George Goring. The house has many historical links. In 1918, it was rented for Prime Minister Lloyd George. It was here in October that year that a meeting of the Imperial War Cabinet agreed a cable should be sent to the United States President Wilson authorising him to proceed with negotiations for an armistice with Germany. The house is now privately owned and run as serviced apartments for retired people.

Bedlam is another name commonly seen, and not just in Sussex. The name is derived from Bethlehem – 'house of bread' – originally a hospital for the poor who were ill or had no home. By the 16th century these hospitals had often become little more than lunatic asylums. The name was shortened to Bedlam and the word assumed a different meaning. In this street is the Pest House, previously an isolation hospital.

The Church of Holy Trinity in Hurstpierpoint was built in 1845. It replaced the ancient Church of St Lawrence, which the Victorians thought too small and old-fashioned. The new building could hold a thousand people, reflecting the importance of church going to the population of this area.

THE WALK

1. From the car park walk towards the library and turn right. Cross the brow of a hill and opposite the Health Centre take the footpath sign left. Enter a large field and swing around the northern edge, with views of Hurstpierpoint College, before meeting a crossing footpath in the woods and here turn right. Walk ahead as the path opens out to become St George's Lane; pass the disused church and on reaching the main road turn right for 30m then cross carefully to climb steps into the woods opposite.

THE BASICS

Distance: 5¼ miles: 8.4 km

Gradient: Gently rolling countryside with very few gradients

Severity: Easy terrain but one of the longest walks in this book, with lots of stiles and some careful navigation required

Approx time to walk: 140 minutes

Stiles: Eighteen

Maps: OS Landranger 198 (Brighton & Lewes); Explorer 122 (Brighton & Hove)

Path description: Mostly open parkland

Start point: Trinity Road car park, Hurstpierpoint, BN6 9UY (Grid Ref. TQ 281165)

Parking: Free disc parking

Dog friendly: Sheep in the fields around Danny

Public toilets: Beside the car park

Nearest food: Vineyard Lodge restaurant/bar or the New Inn

2. This path leads over two stiles down a grassy bank to a tarmac drive. Follow the lane straight ahead towards the downs, passing 'The Granary' on your right. Pass through a metal gate to enter a farm track. After a couple of gates and 'pinch-points' the path goes straight over a tarmac drive, up a small hill and over two stiles to reach a public road.

3. Turn right heading downhill and at a house called 'Bearstakes' turn left to follow the hedge line left over three stiles to reach a crossing footpath. Turn right through a kissing gate. Cross the next field diagonally heading towards Jack and Jill Windmills in the distance. After two more kissing gates take the right fork and at the far side of the field cross a pinch-point into the woods.

4. Turn right then left to reach Coldharbour Farm and here turn right over a stile besides a gate. After one more stile and two pinch-points reach 'Hautboys' and walk past the house on the outside of their fence and then enter the drive through a pinch-point.

5. At the end of the drive turn left on the tarmac road and in just 20m turn right following the footpath fingerpost into the woods. A plank bridge and stile lead into an open field where you may see the alpacas on either side. Two more stiles lead onto the drive at the entrance to the splendid house called 'Danny'. Cross straight over the drive to pass just north of the house.

6. Just before the outbuildings a footpath fingerpost leads over a stile to the right. A further stile, plank bridge and pinch-point lead into an open field where the path forks across the field. Take the left fork heading just left of two large trees. Two more stiles lead into the next field at the far side of which you enter the woods over a stile. Exit over a stile to walk around the edge of a large paddock.

7. At the next crossing footpath turn left and the path soon becomes a driveway passing through the tile-hung houses of Bedlam Street. The driveway (from Randolphs Farm) becomes tarmac and in 100m reaches the main road. Cross carefully straight over and follow the footpath on the far side for 300m to pass through a big gap in the hedge line. Continue along the edges of two more fields to reach a crossing footpath.

8. Turn right to head north and, just after the outbuildings of Wanbarrow Farm,

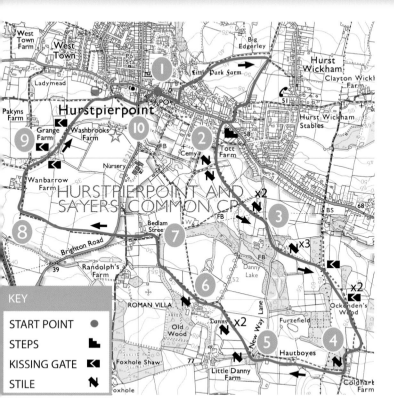

reach a crossroads of paths and here turn right on a wide track to leave a large open field on your right. Take care now because in just 200m the footpath forks left away from the main track onto a grassy path into the trees.

9. Cross a footbridge over a stream and then follow the stream to a kissing gate after which the path heads in the general direction of Hurstpierpoint Church to pass through two more kissing gates before reaching a four-armed fingerpost. Take the bridleway going slightly right to pass just south of the church and reach the main road.

10. Cross carefully to the path opposite and in 50m, at the next footpath junction, turn left along West Furlong Lane to the High Street where a quick left and right turn will lead you back into the car park.

THE ARUN VALLEY

WE HAVE ALLOWED A LITTLE POETIC LICENCE WITH OUR
FINAL WALK — IN THAT IT ONLY BECOMES CIRCULAR BY THE
USE OF A FIVE-MINUTE TRAIN JOURNEY.
BUT DON'T BE PUT OFF!

Soon after the Norman Conquest of 1066, William 1 ordered the building of castles to defend his new realm. Those along the south coast included Lewes, Bramber and Arundel, which protected the estuaries of the three major Sussex rivers – the Ouse, Adur and Arun.

This walk explores the valley of the River Arun as it cuts its way through five miles of the South Downs. What makes the walk so attractive is that there is no public road along the full length of the valley and much of the route is actually by the riverside.

For the best views of Arundel Castle you need to look behind you soon after you join the river. Most of what you see from this viewpoint is attractive 18th & 19th century restoration work, although the castle dates right back to 1070.

It has been the family home of the Dukes of Norfolk and their ancestors for 850 years. The duke holds the title Earl Marshal of England and is responsible for organising royal coronations – a not too onerous duty during the past 60 years!

As you approach Burpham, you will see it is high above the river. In fact, to reach it you must climb Jacobs Ladder or 'the seventy steps'. Tradition has it that these were much used by smugglers in the 18th century bringing their French brandy up the river to hide in the cellars of the inn before later moving it on to the gentlemen's clubs of London.

The path up to St. Mary's Church is named after Marjorie Hay, the daughter of Tickner Edwardes who was vicar of Burpham until 1935. Apparently Marjorie slipped and fell on her way to church one orning and the reverend paid to have the path improved. He was a keen beekeeper and s book 'The Lore of the Honey Bee' is a classic of its kind.

fter crossing the railway for the second time there is a splendid view of South Stoke llage across the river. At the end of a 2½-mile cul-de-sac, it is a delightfully remote ace for the visitor. Its church of St. Leonard is nearly a thousand years old and services e still lit by candlelight.

he path from here to neighbouring North Stoke crosses a splendid new bridge built in 009 by soldiers of the 70 Ghurkha Field Support Squadron. Once in North Stoke you an't miss the smallest tourist information centre in Sussex ... it's the telephone kiosk n the corner of the road!

oughton Bridge is a local beauty spot and, with limited parking, the best way to see it is n foot, or on horseback - as Charles 11 did whilst fleeing to exile after his defeat at the attle of Worcester. There are tales of him taking ale at e George & Dragon Inn, a little way up the hill, before rossing the river to spend the night in Amberley Castle.

ow simply enjoy a little refreshment in the Riverside earoom or the Bridge Inn garden - both delightful.

THE BASICS

istance: 5½ miles: 8.8 km

radient: A mainly flat river walk with one flight of steps and a gentle hill

everity: Moderate/strenuous

pprox time to walk: 150 minutes

tiles: Fourteen

laps: OS Landranger 197 (Chichester & the South Downs); Explorer 121 (Arundel & ulborough)

ath description: Good riverside paths with quiet country lanes but lots of stiles

tart point: Arundel Railway Station, BN18 9PH (Grid Ref. TQ 024064)

arking: Pay & display in station car park

og friendly: Yes but on a lead at start and finish

ublic toilets: At the train station and at the Bridge Inn

earest food: Riverside tearooms or the Bridge Inn or lots back in Arundel town

THE ARUN VALLEY

1. From the station car park walk towards the town. Keep on the left side of the A27 until you reach the pedestrian crossing. Cross here, and continue ahead. Just after the B & B called Portreeves follow a public footpath sign to the right to the river and turn right.

2. Follow the river as it sweeps gracefully left. After 1km the path swings away from the river to a kissing gate and a railway crossing. Cross carefully and immediately after the house turn left following a track into the woods. Follow this to reach a kissing gate and walk ahead with an open field on your right and a line of poplar trees ahead. Cross a dropping stile beneath the trees and walk diagonally across the field to a 'rife'.

3. Turn half right over a concrete bridge and in 30m look for a fingerpost to your left. Cross a stile here, through a gap in the hedge, to follow a path along the right hand side of a field to again reach the bank of the river. Cross a stile up onto the bank and turn right over a second one to follow this 'elbow' of the River Arun. In 100m go left over two stiles crossing a deep rife and a couple of more stiles will lead you to the foot of 'Jacobs Ladder'.

4. Gently climb the steps and at the top follow the enclosed path to walk past Burpham Playing Fields. Pass left of the pavilion to reach the George Inn and (if it's too early for refreshment) continue straight ahead into the churchyard of St Mary's Church.

5. Pass left of the church and emerge onto the tarmac road and continue northward to reach Peppering Farm. At the T-junction here turn left going downhill past the 'cul-de-sac' sign. This becomes a stone track with cottages to the right. At the bottom of the hill turn right over a stile besides a gate to follow the raised bank along the river to two more stiles over the railway. Cross with all due caution and stay on the raised bank as the river sweeps right. After 750m cross a stile into a bushy area and exit over a second stile back onto the riverbank. There is now a lovely view across the river of South Stoke, as you approach an iron bridge with a track leading out of the village.

Cross a stile onto the track and, ignoring the bridge, pass through a kissing gate in front of you to continue on the same side of the river as before. The path curves a little left and in 200m approaches a line of trees to the right. Just before reaching a metal gate on the bank turn right off it, towards these trees, and pass through a kissing gate to enter the woods following a yellow footpath arrow. Walk carefully through the trees, avoiding as much mud as possible, to finally reach a most unexpected and splendid suspension bridge, recently rebuilt by the Ghurkhas.

Cross this footbridge and in a further 50m a kissing gate leads onto an open field and a clear path heading gently uphill. At the top,

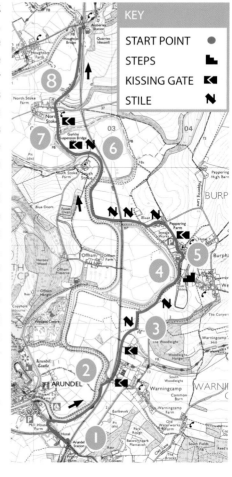

KEY

START POINT	●
STEPS	◣
KISSING GATE	◪
STILE	⋈

pass through two kissing gates to walk behind a row of cottages and emerge onto a tarmac road. Turn left and in just 10m, besides the telephone kiosk, turn immediately right heading northwards and downhill.

Follow this generally quiet lane for just over 1 km (20 minutes) to reach Houghton Bridge with the welcoming sight of the Bridge Inn and the Riverside Tearooms. When suitably refreshed walk along the main road under the railway bridge and turn right into Amberley Station where a regular train service will return you one stop down the line to Arundel.

ABOUT THE AUTHORS

Keith and Sally met more than ten years ago on the Annual South Downs Way Walk and no
jointly organise that event every June. Up to 250 people take part over nine days, walkir
the full 100 miles of the national trail. Now approaching its 35th year, it is one of the longes
established walking events in the country.

Sally took her degree in Economics and Geography at the University of Exeter and went c
to a doctorate in Geography, whilst Keith achieved a 'first' in Engineering at Liverpool befo
joining BEA as a pilot. They are both now retired and as a result are busier than ever.

They regularly write walks in West Sussex for newspapers and magazines and have bee
commissioned to write walks for some of the fine hotels in the county. Together they create
a 39-mile trail called the New Lipchis Way and waymarked the full length before writing th
trail guide. Keith is also co-author of the West Sussex Literary Trail guidebook in which Sa
is acknowledged for 'selflessly volunteering to carry the nails as we waymarked the tra
Both trails now feature on the OS maps of West Sussex.

Today, under the name Footprints of Sussex, they organise a programme of guided wal
throughout the year, in co-operation with their good friends at Per-Rambulations. Althoug
most of these are in West Sussex they do occasionally venture further afield and have le
walks in the New Forest, on the Isle of Wight, in London and even in northern France.

But their declared passion will always be for Kiplings's 'blunt, bow-headed whale-back
downs' of Sussex.

To visit their website go to www.footprintsofsussex.co.uk.